Guitar Chords

Easy-to-Use, Easy-to-Carry

One Chord on EVERY Page

Edited by
Jake Jackson

D0150831

Fast Learn Guitar

**FLAME TREE
PUBLISHING**

Produced and created by
FLAME TREE PUBLISHING
Crabtree Hall, Crabtree Lane
Fulham, London, SW6 6TY
United Kingdom
www.flametreepublishing.com

See our music information site:
www.musicfirebox.com

First Published in 2006

Publisher & Creative Director: Nick Wells
Editor: Sarah Goulding
Designer: Mike Spender

10 09

15

Flame Tree Publishing is part of the
Foundry Creative Media Company Limited

Contents

As a guitarist, even if you only ever play single-note solos, it is essential that you know your chords – they are the building blocks behind all musical compositions. The main part of the book provides one chord per page for easy reference, with a variety of positions and fingerings for hundreds of chords.

Use the tabs on the side of each page to find the chord you want quickly.

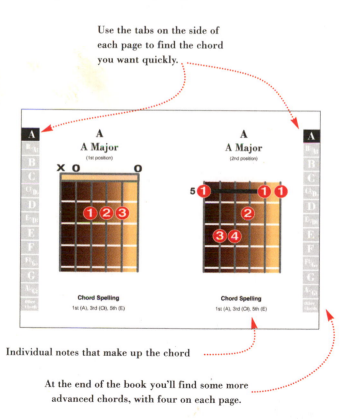

Individual notes that make up the chord

At the end of the book you'll find some more advanced chords, with four on each page.

How to Use
the Chord Boxes

The chord fretboxes in this book will help you to learn the shapes of hundreds of chords, and will be a useful reference guide when you are playing and composing your own music. This is by no means a comprehensive manual, but should provide enough chord formations to keep even the most advanced musicians busy!

• While it might seem dull learning the fingerings, remember that the wider your chord vocabulary becomes, the more you will be able to vary your playing style and compositions. It is particularly important to know your chords if you are planning to jam with other musicians – when the leader shouts out "E!", you don't want to be left high and dry wondering where the chord might be while the other musicians sail off into the next verse.

- The chords are divided by key, from A to G$_\sharp$, with the key's notes shown at the top of the page. The left-hand pages outline the main chords you will need to learn, each shown in three different fingerings or positions. It can be useful to know a variety of positions for each chord, especially when fitting them into a progression – when you are playing in high fingerboard positions, you do not want to have to stop and scrabble around trying to find a chord position back on the first few frets.

- The right-hand pages show some of the more advanced chords that can be handy when playing progressions, for linking chords or for use in improvisations. There are only two positions shown for these, in order to include a greater variety of chords.

- The diagrams show the guitar fretboard in an upright position, with high E on the right. The nut appears at the top if the chord is played on the lower frets. If the chord is in a higher position, the fret number on which it begins is given to the left of the diagram.

- The notes to be played are shown as circles, with the finger number that should be used for each note (1 = index finger; 2 = middle finger; 3 = ring finger; 4 = little finger). An X above the string denotes that the string should not be played in the chord and should be muted, to prevent it sounding accidentally. An O above the string shows that it should be played as an open string.

- We have tried to make this chord section as easy to use as possible, so where there is a choice of note name (e.g. F♯ or G♭) we have selected the one that you are most likely to come across in your playing.

- Where a chord contains a flattened (♭) or sharpened (♯) interval (e.g. ♯5ᵗʰ), you can find the notes by playing a fret lower (for a flat) or a fret higher (for a sharp) than the interval note indicated at the top of the page. In the keys that contain a large number of sharps or flats, double flats (♭♭) and double sharps (x) sometimes occur in the augmented and diminished chords. A double flat is the notes two frets below the named note, while a double sharp is two frets up.

An X at the top of a string indicates that this string should not be played

An O at the top of the string means that this should be played as an open string

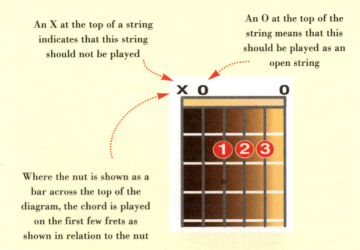

Where the nut is shown as a bar across the top of the diagram, the chord is played on the first few frets as shown in relation to the nut

Where a bar appears between notes, the specified finger should hold down the notes across the strings shown

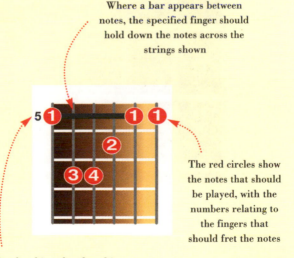

The red circles show the notes that should be played, with the numbers relating to the fingers that should fret the notes

Where the chord is to be played in a different position, the fret number is shown to the left of the diagram

B♭/A♯
B
C
C♯/D♭
D
E♭/D♯
E
F
F♯/G♭
G
A♭/G♯
Other Chords

A

A Major

(1st position)

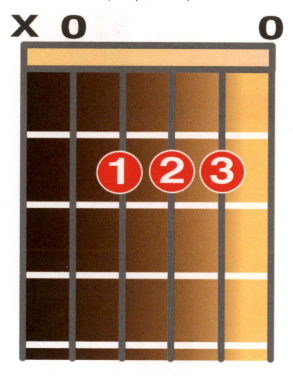

Chord Spelling

1st (A), 3rd (C♯), 5th (E)

A
A Major
(2nd position)

A
B♭/A♯
B
C
C♯/D♭
D
E♭/D♯
E
F
F♯/G♭
G
A♭/G♯
Other Chords

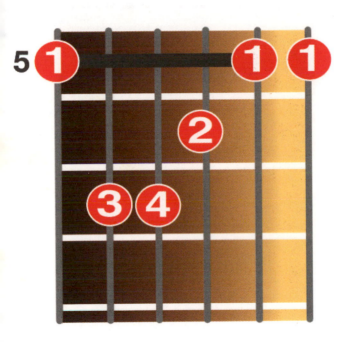

5 1 ... 1 1
2
3 4

Chord Spelling
1st (A), 3rd (C♯), 5th (E)

Bb/A#

B

C

C#/Db

D

Eb/D#

E

F

F#/Gb

G

Ab/G#

Other Chords

Am
A Minor

(1st position)

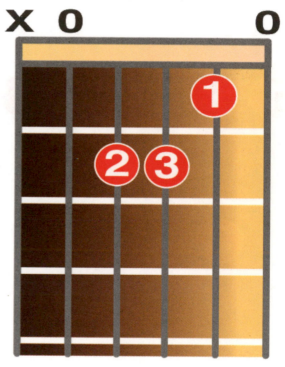

Chord Spelling

1st (A), b3rd (C), 5th (E)

Am
A Minor

(2nd position)

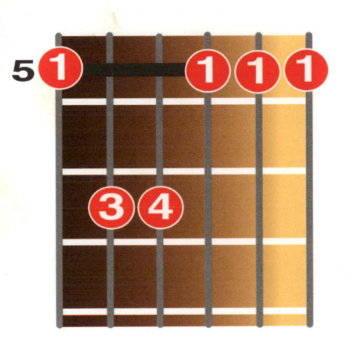

5

B♭/A♯

B

C

C♯/D♭

D

E♭/D♯

E

F

F♯/G♭

G

A♭/G♯

Other Chords

Chord Spelling

1st (A), ♭3rd (C), 5th (E)

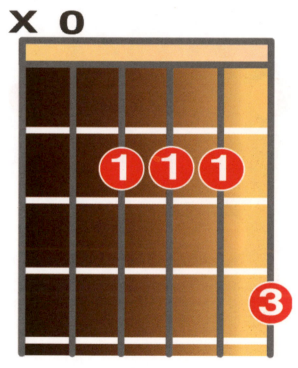

Amaj7
A Major 7th

(1st position)

Chord Spelling
1st (A), 3rd (C#), 5th (E), 7th (G#)

A
B♭/A#
B
C
C#/D♭
D
E♭/D#
E
F
F#/G♭
G
A♭/G#
Other Chords

Amaj7
A Major 7th

(2nd position)

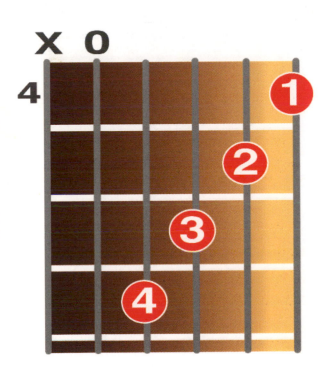

Chord Spelling

1st (A), 3rd (C#), 5th (E), 7th (G#)

A

B♭/A#

B

C

C#/D♭

D

E♭/D#

E

F

F#/G♭

G

A♭/G#

Other Chords

Am7
A Minor 7th

(1st position)

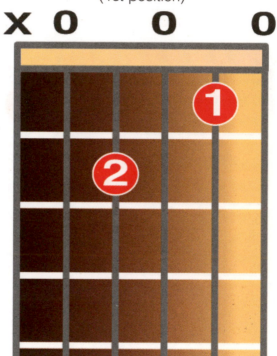

Chord Spelling

1st (A), ♭3rd (C), 5th (E), ♭7th (G)

Am7
A Minor 7th

(2nd position)

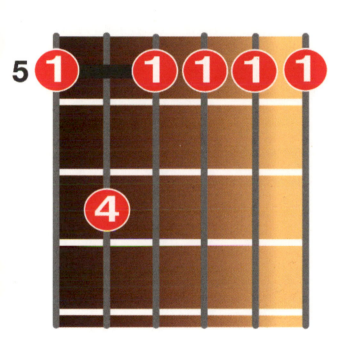

5

A

B♭/A♯

B

C

C♯/D♭

D

E♭/D♯

E

F

F♯/G♭

G

A♭/G♯

Other Chords

Chord Spelling

1st (A), ♭3rd (C), 5th (E), ♭7th (G)

A
B♭/A♯
B
C
C♯/D♭
D
E♭/D♯
E
F
F♯/G♭
G
A♭/G♯
Other Chords

Asus4
A Suspended 4th

(1st position)

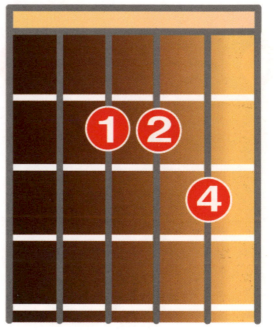

Chord Spelling

1st (A), 4th (D), 5th (E)

Asus4
A Suspended 4th
(2nd position)

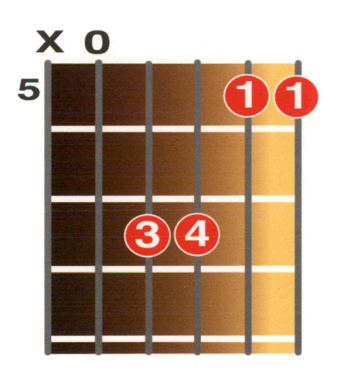

Chord Spelling
1st (A), 4th (D), 5th (E)

A

B♭/A♯

B

C

C♯/D♭

D

E♭/D♯

E

F

F♯/G♭

G

A♭/G♯

Other Chords

A
B♭/A♯
B
C
C♯/D♭
D
E♭/D♯
E
F
F♯/G♭
G
A♭/G♯
Other Chords

A7sus4
A Dominant 7th sus4

(1st position)

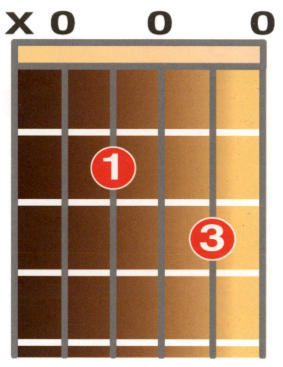

Chord Spelling

1st (A), 4th (D), 5th (E), ♭7th (G)

A7sus4
A Dominant 7th sus4

(2nd position)

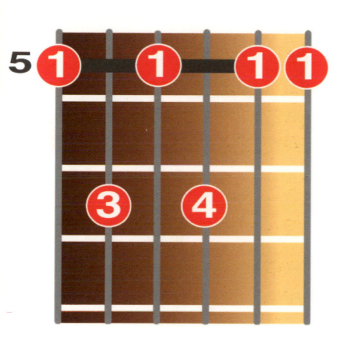

A
Bb/A#
B
C
C#/Db
D
Eb/D#
E
F
F#/Gb
G
Ab/G#
Other Chords

Chord Spelling

1st (A), 4th (D), 5th (E), b7th (G)

A

B♭/A♯

B

C

C♯/D♭

D

E♭/D♯

E

F

F♯/G♭

G

A♭/G♯

Other Chords

A6
A Major 6th

(1st position)

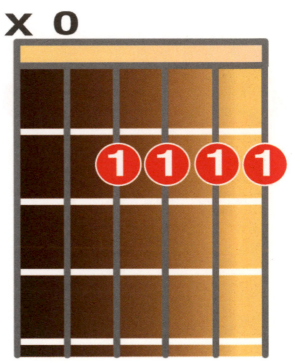

Chord Spelling

1st (A), 3rd (C♯), 5th (E), 6th (F♯)

A6
A Major 6th
(2nd position)

A

B♭/A♯

B

C

C♯/D♭

D

E♭/D♯

E

F

F♯/G♭

G

A♭/G♯

Other Chords

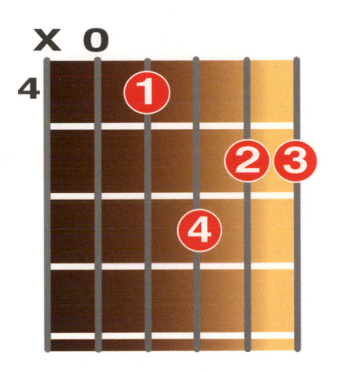

X O

4

1 2 3 4

Chord Spelling
1st (A), 3rd (C♯), 5th (E), 6th (F♯)

Am6
A Minor 6th

(1st position)

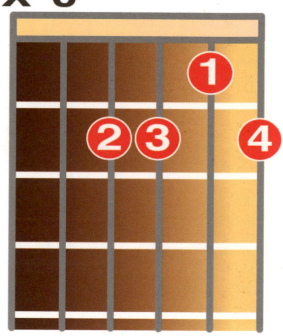

Chord Spelling

1st (A), ♭3rd (C), 5th (E), 6th (F#)

A
B♭/A♯
B
C
C♯/D♭
D
E♭/D♯
E
F
F♯/G♭
G
A♭/G♯
Other Chords

Am6
A Minor 6th

(2nd position)

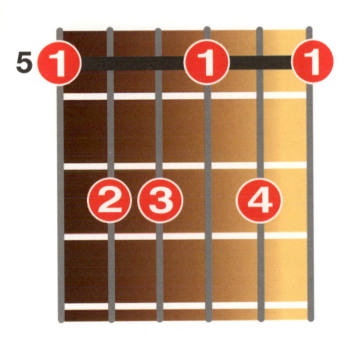

A

B♭/A♯

B

C

C♯/D♭

D

E♭/D♯

E

F

F♯/G♭

G

A♭/G♯

Other Chords

Chord Spelling

1st (A), ♭3rd (C), 5th (E), 6th (F♯)

A7
A Dominant 7th

(1st position)

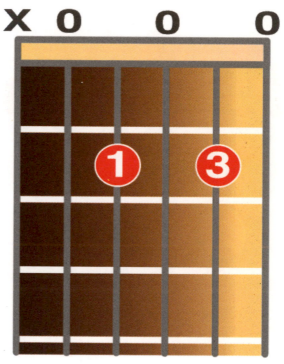

Chord Spelling

1st (A), 3rd (C#), 5th (E), ♭7th (G)

A
B♭/A#
B
C
C#/D♭
D
E♭/D#
E
F
F#/G♭
G
A♭/G#
Other Chords

A7
A Dominant 7th
(2nd position)

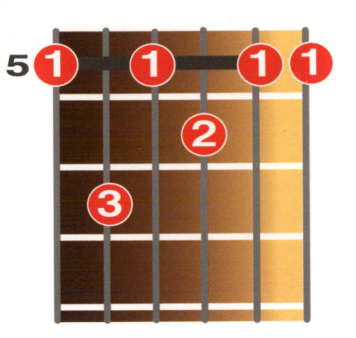

A

Bb/A#

B

C

C#/Db

D

Eb/D#

E

F

F#/Gb

G

Ab/G#

Other Chords

Chord Spelling

1st (A), 3rd (C#), 5th (E), b7th (G)

A9
A Dominant 9th

(1st position)

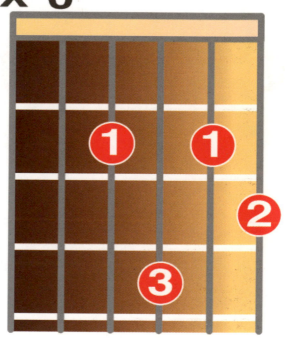

Chord Spelling

1st (A), 3rd (C#), 5th (E), ♭7th (G), 9th (B)

A9
A Dominant 9th
(2nd position)

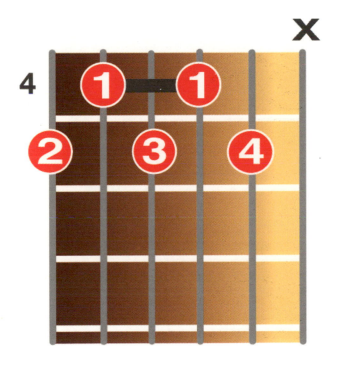

A

B♭/A♯

B

C

C♯/D♭

D

E♭/D♯

E

F

F♯/G♭

G

A♭/G♯

Other Chords

Chord Spelling

1st (A), 3rd (C♯), 5th (E), ♭7th (G), 9th (B)

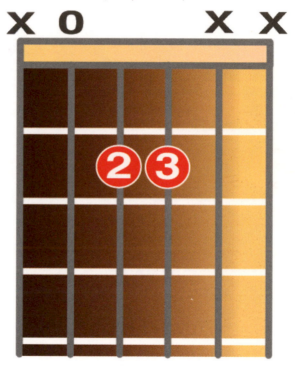

A
B♭/A♯
B
C
C♯/D♭
D
E♭/D♯
E
F
F♯/G♭
G
A♭/G♯
Other Chords

A5

A 5th 'power chord'

(1st position)

Chord Spelling

1st (A), 5th (E)

$A^6{}_9$
A Major 6th add 9th

(1st position)

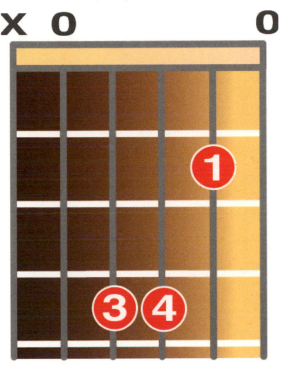

Chord Spelling

1st (A), 3rd (C#), 5th (E), 6th (F#), 9th (B)

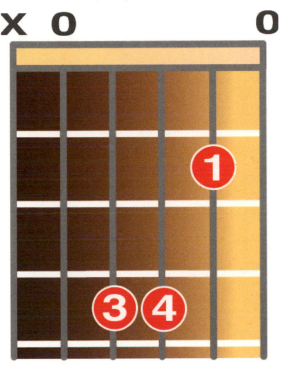

A
Bb/A#
B
C
C#/Db
D
Eb/D#
E
F
F#/Gb
G
Ab/G#
Other Chords

A11

A Dominant 11th

(1st position)

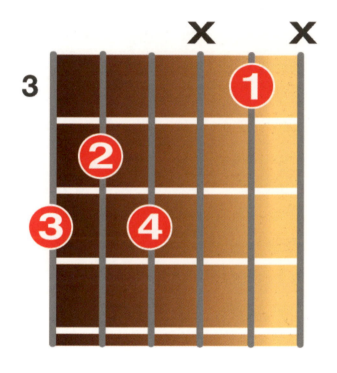

Chord Spelling

1st (A), 3rd (C♯), 5th (E), ♭7th (G), 9th (B), 11th (D)

A13
A Dominant 13th
(1st position)

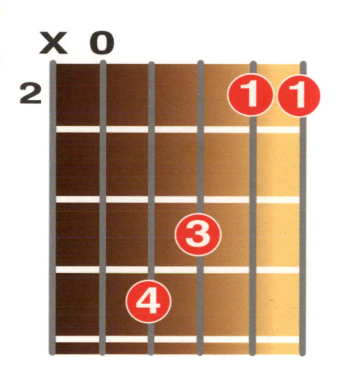

A

B♭/A♯

B

C

C♯/D♭

D

E♭/D♯

E

F

F♯/G♭

G

A♭/G♯

Other Chords

Chord Spelling

st (A), 3rd (C♯), 5th (E), ♭7th (G), 9th (B), 13th (F♯)

B♭/A♯

B

C

C♯/D♭

D

E♭/D♯

E

F

F♯/G♭

G

A♭/G♯

Other Chords

Aadd9
A Major add 9th

(1st position)

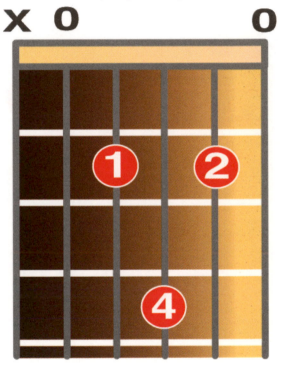

Chord Spelling

1st (A), 3rd (C♯), 5th (E), 9th (B)

Am9
A Minor 9th
(1st position)

X O

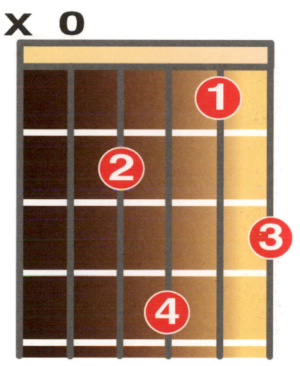

Chord Spelling

1st (A), ♭3rd (C), 5th (E), ♭7th (G), 9th (B)

A
B♭/A♯
B
C
C♯/D♭
D
E♭/D♯
E
F
F♯/G♭
G
A♭/G♯
Other Chords

B♭/A#
B
C
C#/D♭
D
E♭/D#
E
F
F#/G♭
G
A♭/G#
Other Chords

Amaj9
A Major 9th

(1st position)

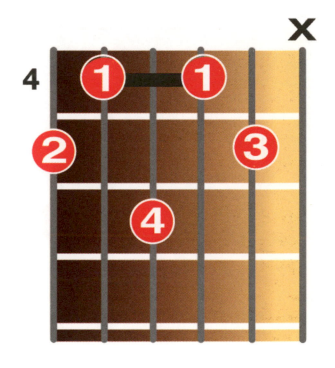

4

X

Chord Spelling
1st (A), 3rd (C#), 5th (E), 7th (G#), 9th (B)

A+
A Augmented
(1st position)

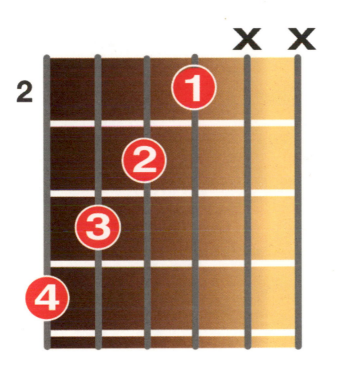

2

X X

A
Bb/A#
B
C
C#/Db
D
Eb/D#
E
F
F#/Gb
G
Ab/G#
Other Chords

Chord Spelling
1st (A), 3rd (C#), #5th (E#)

A⁰⁷

A Diminished 7th

(1st position)

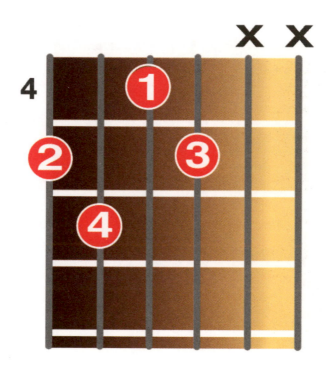

Chord Spelling

1st (A), ♭3rd (C), ♭5th (E♭), ♭♭7th (G♭)

A
B♭/A♯
B
C
C♯/D♭
D
E♭/D♯
E
F
F♯/G♭
G
A♭/G♯
Other Chords

A⁰
A Diminished triad

(1st position)

A
B♭/A♯
B
C
C♯/D♭
D
E♭/D♯
E
F
F♯/G♭
G
A♭/G♯
Other Chords

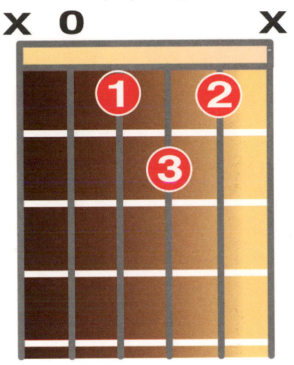

Chord Spelling

1st (A), ♭3rd (C), ♭5th (E♭)

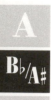

B♭

B♭ Major

(1st position)

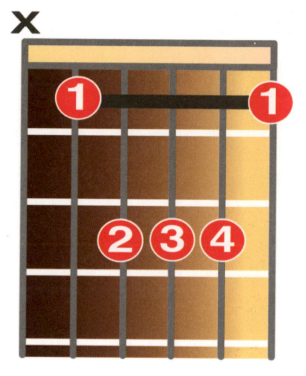

Chord Spelling

1st (B♭), 3rd (D), 5th (F)

B♭

B♭ Major

(2nd position)

A

B♭/A♯

B

C

C♯/D♭

D

E♭/D♯

E

F

F♯/G♭

G

A♭/G♯

Other Chords

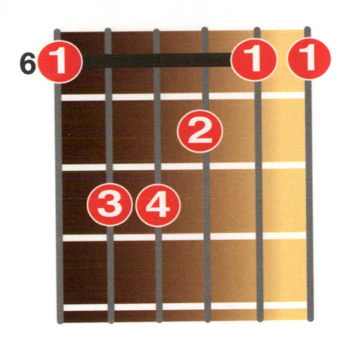

Chord Spelling

1st (B♭), 3rd (D), 5th (F)

B♭m

B♭ Minor

(1st position)

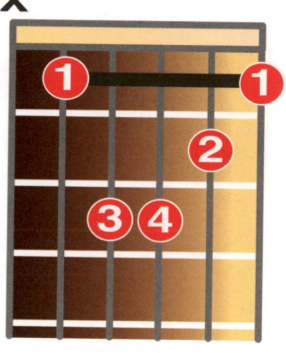

Chord Spelling

1st (B♭), ♭3rd (D♭), 5th (F)

B♭m
B♭ Minor
(2nd position)

A

B♭/A♯

B

C

C♯/D♭

D

E♭/D♯

E

F

F♯/G♭

G

A♭/G♯

Other Chords

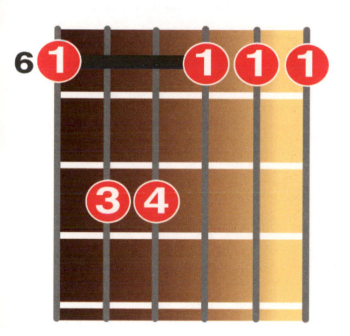

Chord Spelling

1st (B♭), ♭3rd (D♭), 5th (F)

B♭maj7
B♭ Major 7th

(1st position)

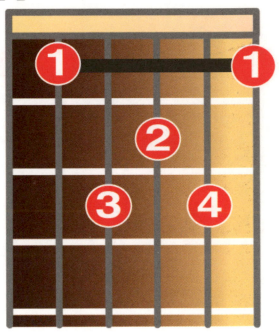

Chord Spelling

1st (B♭), 3rd (D), 5th (F), 7th (A)

B♭maj7
B♭ Major 7th
(2nd position)

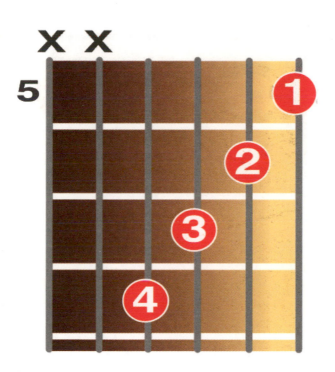

Chord Spelling

1st (B♭), 3rd (D), 5th (F), 7th (A)

A
B♭/A♯
B
C
C♯/D♭
D
E♭/D♯
E
F
F♯/G♭
G
A♭/G♯
Other Chords

B♭m7
B♭ Minor 7th

(1st position)

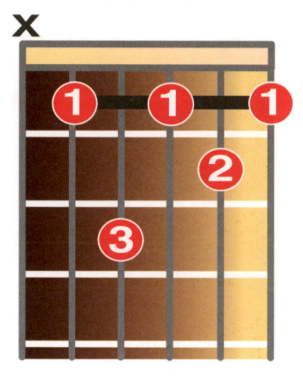

Chord Spelling

1st (B♭), ♭3rd (D♭), 5th (F), ♭7th (A♭)

B♭m7
B♭ Minor 7th

(2nd position)

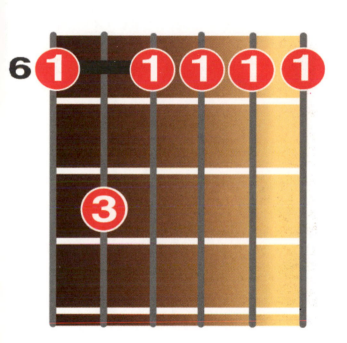

A
B♭/A#
B
C
C#/D♭
D
E♭/D#
E
F
F#/G♭
G
A♭/G#
Other Chords

Chord Spelling

1st (B♭), ♭3rd (D♭), 5th (F), ♭7th (A♭)

B♭sus4

B♭ Suspended 4th

(1st position)

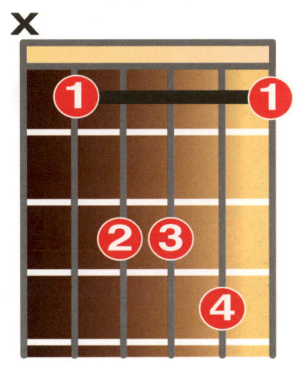

Chord Spelling

1st (B♭), 4th (E♭), 5th (F)

B♭sus4
B♭ Suspended 4th

(2nd position)

A

B♭/A♯

B

C

C♯/D♭

D

E♭/D♯

E

F

F♯/G♭

G

A♭/G♯

Other
Chords

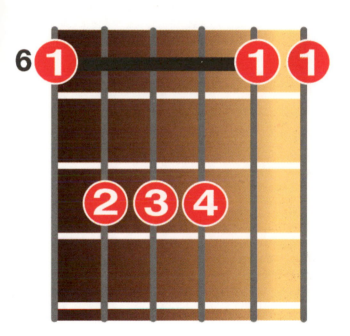

Chord Spelling

1st (B♭), 4th (E♭), 5th (F)

B♭7sus4

B♭ Dominant 7th sus4

(1st position)

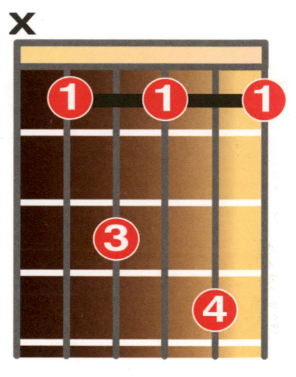

Chord Spelling

1st (B♭), 4th (E♭), 5th (F), ♭7th (A♭)

B♭7sus4
B♭ Dominant 7th sus4

(2nd position)

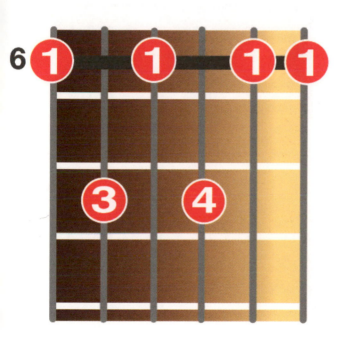

A
B♭/A♯
B
C♯/D♭
D
E♭/D♯
E
F
F♯/G♭
G
A♭/G♯
Other Chords

Chord Spelling

1st (B♭), 4th (E♭), 5th (F), ♭7th (A♭)

B♭6
B♭ Major 6th
(1st position)

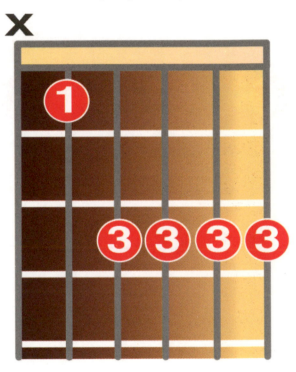

Chord Spelling
1st (B♭), 3rd (D), 5th (F), 6th (G)

B♭6
B♭ Major 6th
(2nd position)

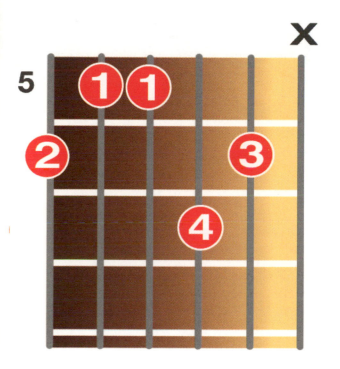

A

B♭/A#

B

C

C#/D♭

D

E♭/D#

E

F

F#/G♭

G

A♭/G#

Other Chords

Chord Spelling
1st (B♭), 3rd (D), 5th (F), 6th (G)

B♭m6
B♭ Minor 6th
(1st position)

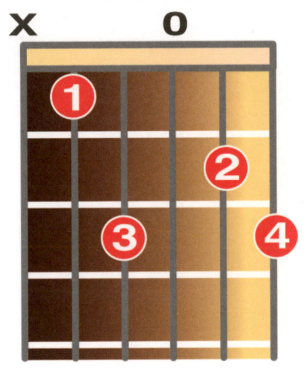

Chord Spelling
1st (B♭), ♭3rd (D♭), 5th (F), 6th (G)

B♭m6
B♭ Minor 6th
(2nd position)

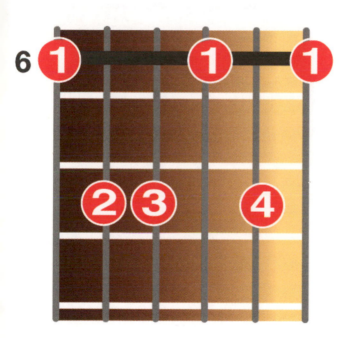

A

B♭/A#

B

C

C#/D♭

D

E♭/D#

E

F

F#/G♭

G

A♭/G#

Other Chords

Chord Spelling

1st (B♭), ♭3rd (D♭), 5th (F), 6th (G)

B♭7

B♭ Dominant 7th

(1st position)

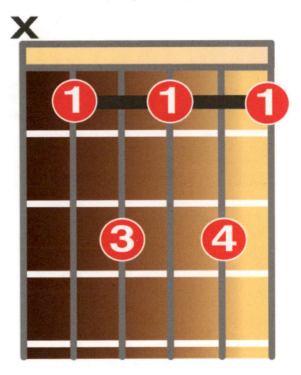

A
B♭/A♯
B
C
C♯/D♭
D
E♭/D♯
E
F
F♯/G♭
G
A♭/G♯
Other Chords

Chord Spelling

1st (B♭), 3rd (D), 5th (F), ♭7th (A♭)

B♭7
B♭ Dominant 7th
(2nd position)

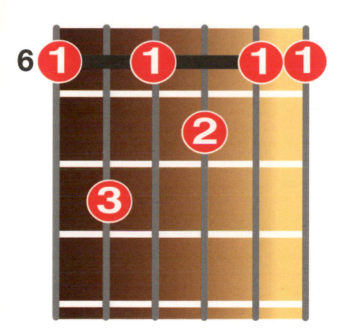

6

A

B♭/A#

B

C

C#/D♭

D

E♭/D#

E

F

F#/G♭

G

A♭/G#

Other Chords

Chord Spelling

1st (B♭), 3rd (D), 5th (F), ♭7th (A♭)

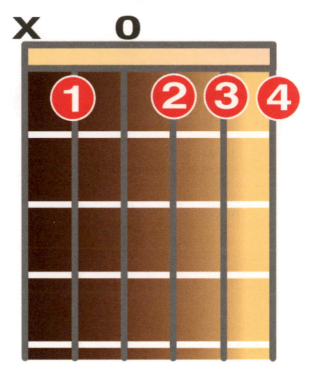

B♭9

B♭ Dominant 9th

(1st position)

Chord Spelling

1st (B♭), 3rd (D), 5th (F), ♭7th (A♭), 9th (C)

A

B♭/A♯

B

C

C♯/D♭

D

E♭/D♯

E

F

F♯/G♭

G

A♭/G♯

Other
Chords

B♭9

B♭ Dominant 9th

(2nd position)

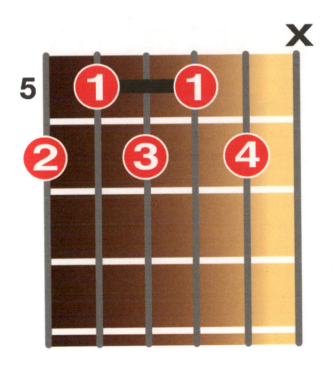

Chord Spelling

1st (B♭), 3rd (D), 5th (F), ♭7th (A♭), 9th (C)

A

B♭/A♯

B

C

C♯/D♭

D

E♭/D♯

E

F

F♯/G♭

G

A♭/G♯

Other Chords

A

B♭/A♯

B

C

C♯/D♭

D

E♭/D♯

E

F

F♯/G♭

G

A♭/G♯

Other
Chords

B♭5

B♭ 5th 'power chord'

(1st position)

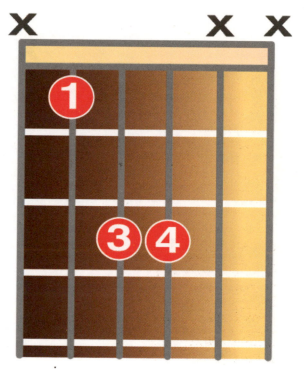

Chord Spelling

1st (B♭), 5th (F)

B♭⁶₉

B♭ Major 6th add 9th

(1st position)

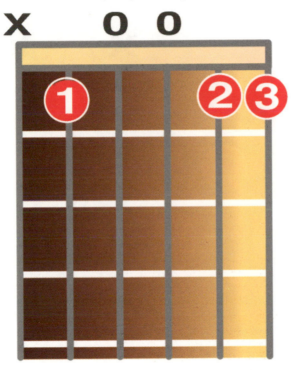

A
B♭/A#
B
C
C#/D♭
D
E♭/D#
E
F
F#/G♭
G
A♭/G#
Other Chords

Chord Spelling

1st (B♭), 3rd (D), 5th (F), 6th (G), 9th (C)

B♭11
B♭ Dominant 11th
(1st position)

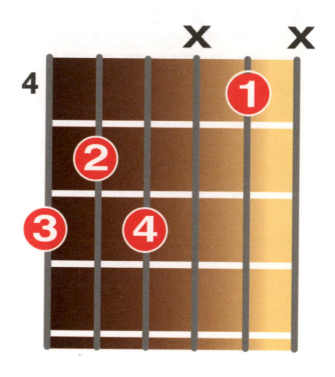

Chord Spelling
1st (B♭), 3rd (D), 5th (F), ♭7th (A♭), 9th (C), 11th (E♭)

B♭13
B♭ Dominant 13th
(1st position)

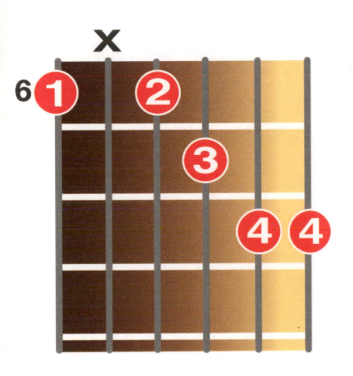

Chord Spelling
1st (B♭), 3rd (D), 5th (F), ♭7th (A♭), 9th (C), 13th (G)

A
B♭/A#
B
C
C#/D♭
D
E♭/D#
E
F
F#/G♭
G
A♭/G#
Other Chords

B♭add9
B♭ Major add 9th
(1st position)

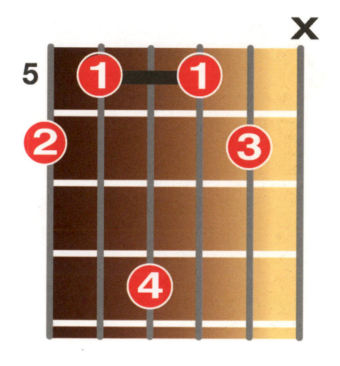

Chord Spelling

1st (B♭), 3rd (D), 5th (F), 9th (C)

B♭m9
B♭ Minor 9th

(1st position)

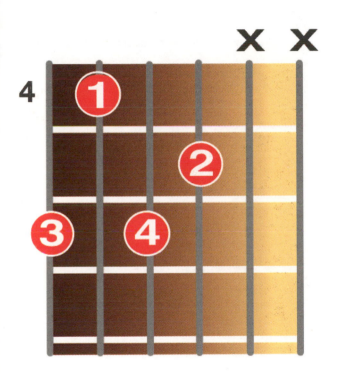

A
B♭/A♯
B
C
C♯/D♭
D
E♭/D♯
E
F
F♯/G♭
G
A♭/G♯
Other Chords

Chord Spelling

1st (B♭), ♭3rd (D♭), 5th (F), ♭7th (A♭), 9th (C)

A

B♭/A#

B

C

C#/D♭

D

E♭/D#

E

F

F#/G♭

G

A♭/G#

Other
Chords

B♭maj9
B♭ Major 9th

(1st position)

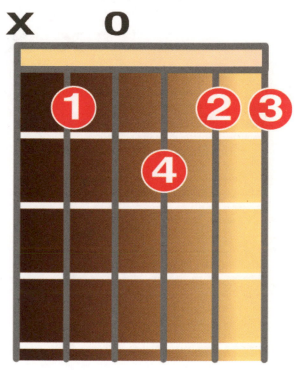

Chord Spelling

1st (B♭), 3rd (D), 5th (F), 7th (A), 9th (C)

B♭+
B♭ Augmented
(1st position)

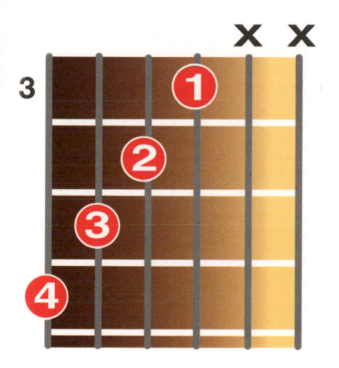

A

B♭/A♯

B

C

C♯/D♭

D

E♭/D♯

E

F

F♯/G♭

G

A♭/G♯

Other Chords

Chord Spelling
1st (B♭), 3rd (D), #5th (F♯)

A

B♭/A♯

B

C

C♯/D♭

D

E♭/D♯

E

F

F♯/G♭

G

A♭/G♯

Other Chords

B♭⁰⁷

B♭ Diminished 7th

(1st position)

X   O   O

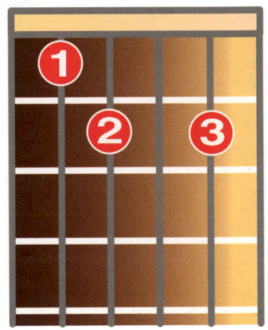

Chord Spelling

1st (B♭), ♭3rd (D♭), ♭5th (F♭), ♭♭7th (A♭♭)

B♭⁰

B♭ Diminished triad

(1st position)

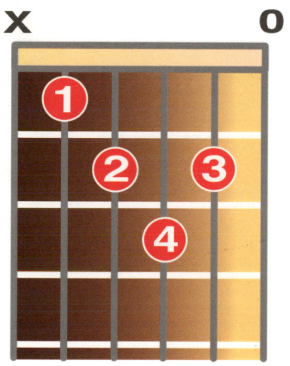

Chord Spelling

1st (B♭), ♭3rd (D♭), ♭5th (F♭)

A

B♭/A♯

B

C

C♯/D♭

D

E♭/D♯

E

F

F♯/G♭

G

A♭/G♯

Other Chords

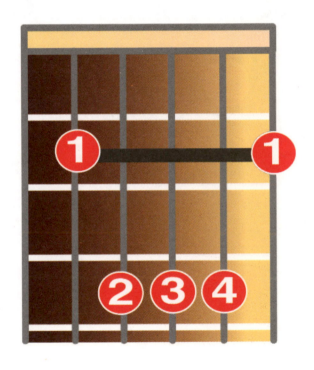

B
B Major
(1st position)

Chord Spelling
1st (B), 3rd (D♯), 5th (F♯)

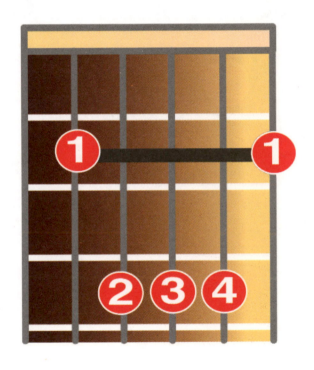

A
B♭/A♯
B
C
C♯/D♭
D
E♭/D♯
E
F
F♯/G♭
G
A♭/G♯
Other Chords

B

B Major

(2nd position)

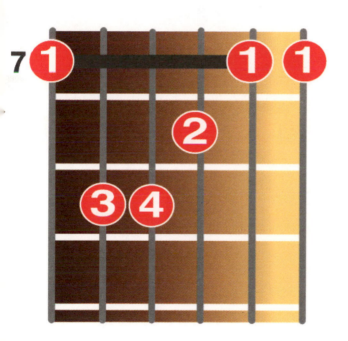

7

A
Bb/A#
B
C
C#/Db
D
Eb/D#
E
F
F#/Gb
G
Ab/G#
Other Chords

Chord Spelling

1st (B), 3rd (D#), 5th (F#)

Bm
B Minor
(1st position)

A
B♭/A♯
B
C
C♯/D♭
D
E♭/D♯
E
F
F♯/G♭
G
A♭/G♯
Other Chords

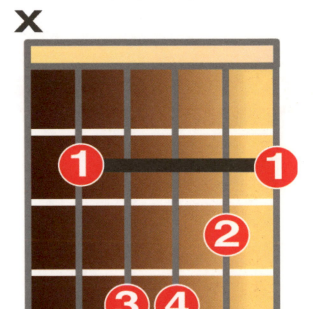

Chord Spelling
1st (B), ♭3rd (D), 5th (F♯)

Bm
B Minor
(2nd position)

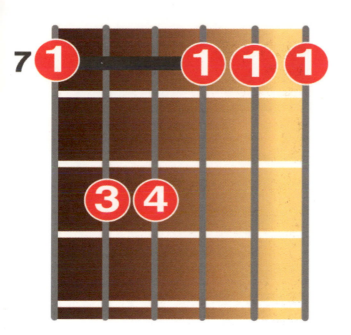

A
B♭/A♯
B
C
C♯/D♭
D
E♭/D♯
E
F
F♯/G♭
G
A♭/G♯
Other Chords

Chord Spelling
1st (B), ♭3rd (D), 5th (F♯)

Bmaj7
B Major 7th

(1st position)

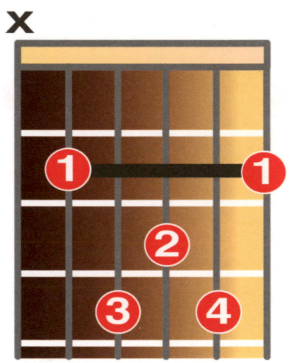

Chord Spelling
1st (B), 3rd (D#), 5th (F#), 7th (A#)

Bmaj7
B Major 7th
(2nd position)

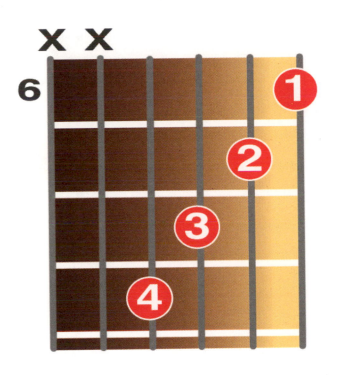

Chord Spelling
1st (B), 3rd (D#), 5th (F#), 7th (A#)

A
Bb/A#
B
C
C#/Db
D
Eb/D#
E
F
F#/Gb
G
Ab/G#
Other Chords

A

B♭/A♯

B

C

C♯/D♭

D

E♭/D♯

E

F

F♯/G♭

G

A♭/G♯

Other
Chords

Bm7
B Minor 7th
(1st position)

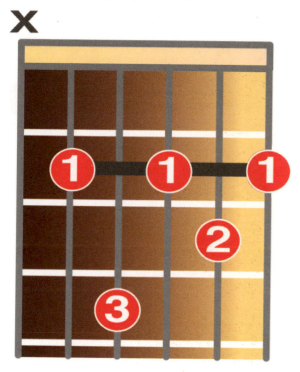

Chord Spelling
1st (B), ♭3rd (D), 5th (F♯), 7th (A)

Bm7
B Minor 7th
(2nd position)

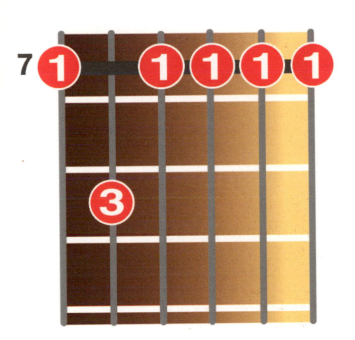

A
B♭/A♯
B
C
C♯/D♭
D
E♭/D♯
E
F
F♯/G♭
G
A♭/G♯
Other Chords

Chord Spelling

1st (B), ♭3rd (D), 5th (F♯), 7th (A)

Bsus4
B Suspended 4th
(1st position)

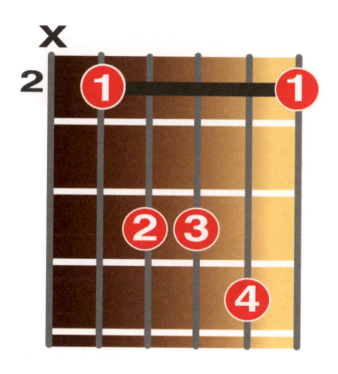

Chord Spelling
1st (B), 4th (E), 5th (F♯)

A
B♭/A♯
B
C
C♯/D♭
D
E♭/D♯
E
F
F♯/G♭
G
A♭/G♯
Other Chords

Bsus4
B Suspended 4th

(2nd position)

A

B♭/A♯

B

C

C♯/D♭

D

E♭/D♯

E

F

F♯/G♭

G

A♭/G♯

Other Chords

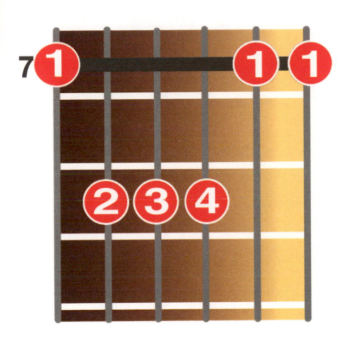

7

Chord Spelling

1st (B), 4th (E), 5th (F♯)

B7sus4
B Dominant 7th sus4

(1st position)

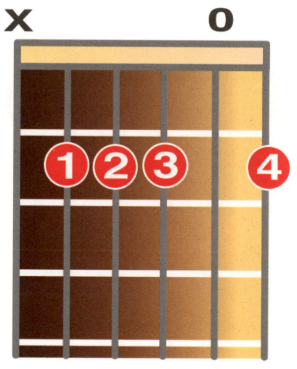

Chord Spelling

1st (B), 4th (E), 5th (F#), ♭7th (A)

B7sus4

B Dominant 7th sus4

(2nd position)

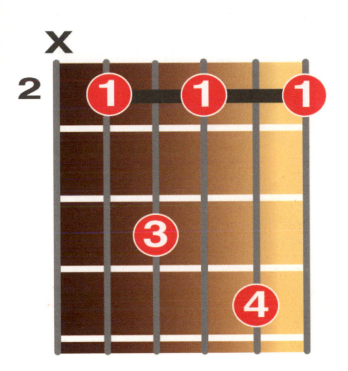

A
B♭/A♯
B
C
C♯/D♭
D
E♭/D♯
E
F
F♯/G♭
G
A♭/G♯
Other Chords

Chord Spelling

1st (B), 4th (E), 5th (F♯), ♭7th (A)

B6
B Major 6th
(1st position)

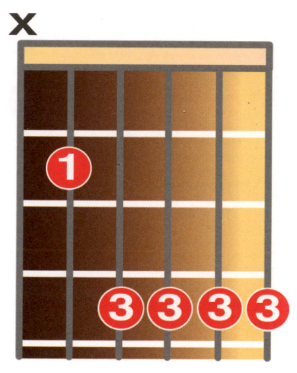

Chord Spelling

1st (B), 3rd (D#), 5th (F#), 6th (G#)

B6
B Major 6th
(2nd position)

A
B♭/A♯
B
C
C♯/D♭
D
E♭/D♯
E
F
F♯/G♭
G
A♭/G♯
Other Chords

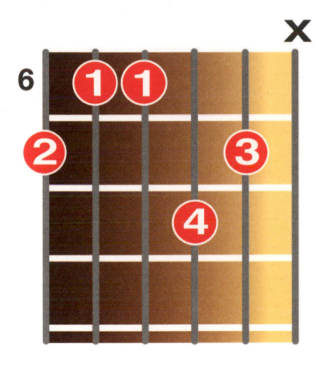

6

X

Chord Spelling
1st (B), 3rd (D♯), 5th (F♯), 6th (G♯)

Bm6
B Minor 6th
(1st position)

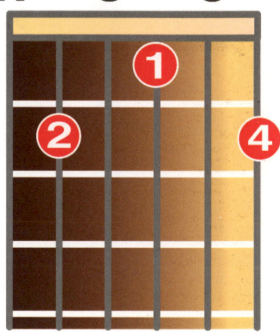

Chord Spelling
1st (B), ♭3rd (D), 5th (F♯), 6th (G♯)

Bm6
B Minor 6th
(2nd position)

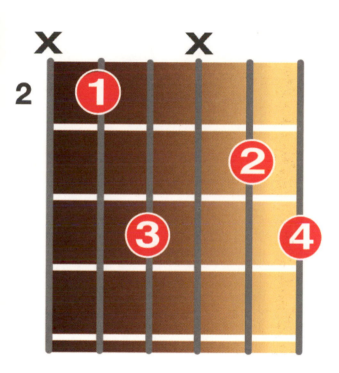

A
B♭/A♯
B
C
C♯/D♭
D
E♭/D♯
E
F
F♯/G♭
G
A♭/G♯
Other Chords

Chord Spelling
1st (B), ♭3rd (D), 5th (F♯), 6th (G♯)

B7
B Dominant 7th
(1st position)

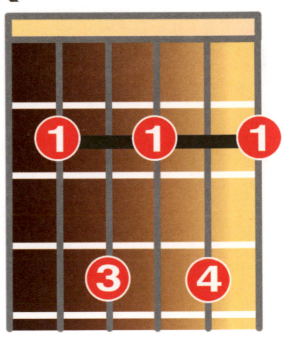

Chord Spelling
1st (B), 3rd (D♯), 5th (F♯), ♭7th (A)

B7

B Dominant 7th

(2nd position)

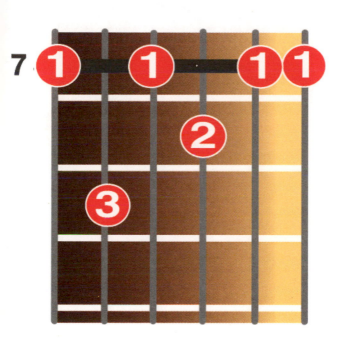

A

B♭/A♯

B

C

C♯/D♭

D

E♭/D♯

E

F

F♯/G♭

G

A♭/G♯

Other Chords

Chord Spelling

1st (B), 3rd (D♯), 5th (F♯), ♭7th (A)

B9
B Dominant 9th
(1st position)

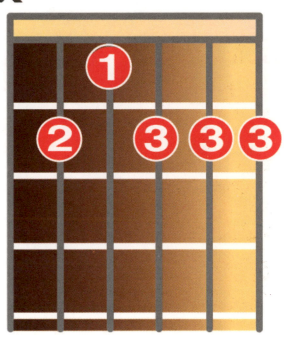

Chord Spelling
1st (B), 3rd (D#), 5th (F#), ♭7th (A), 9th (C#)

A

B♭/A#

B

C

C#/D♭

D

E♭/D#

E

F

F#/G♭

G

A♭/G#

Other
Chords

B9
B Dominant 9th
(2nd position)

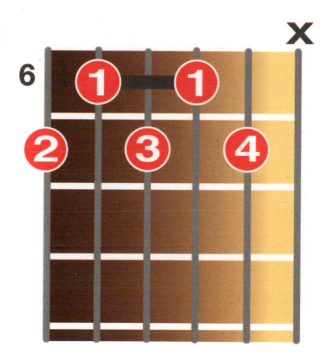

6

X

A
B♭/A♯
B
C
C♯/D♭
D
E♭/D♯
E
F
F♯/G♭
G
A♭/G♯
Other Chords

Chord Spelling
1st (B), 3rd (D♯), 5th (F♯), ♭7th (A), 9th (C♯)

B5

B 5th 'power chord'

(1st position)

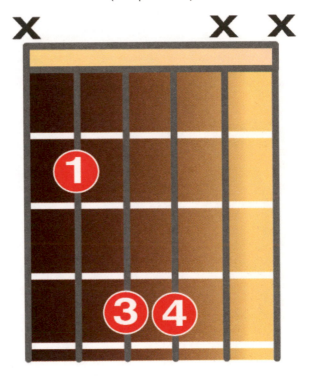

Chord Spelling

1st (B), 5th (F#)

B⁶₉

B Major 6th add 9th

(1st position)

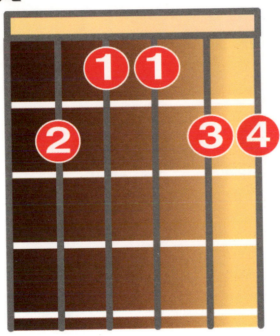

Chord Spelling

1st (B), 3rd (D#), 5th (F#), 6th (G#), 9th (C#)

A

Bb/A#

B

C

C#/Db

D

Eb/D#

E

F

F#/Gb

G

Ab/G#

Other Chords

B11

B Dominant 11th

(1st position)

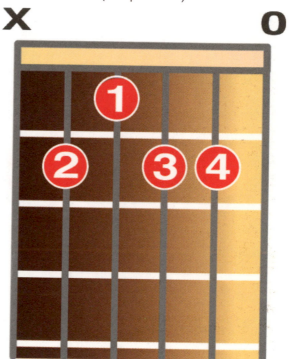

X   O

Chord Spelling

1st (B), 3rd (D#), 5th (F#), ♭7th (A), 9th (C#), 11th (E)

B13

B Dominant 13th

(1st position)

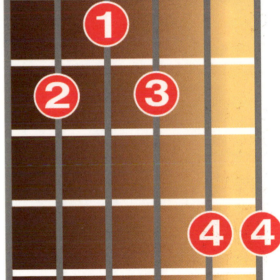

A

B♭/A♯

B

C

C♯/D♭

D

E♭/D♯

E

F

F♯/G♭

G

A♭/G♯

Other Chords

Chord Spelling

1st (B), 3rd (D♯), 5th (F♯), ♭7th (A), 9th (C♯), 13th (G♯)

Badd9
B Major add 9th
(1st position)

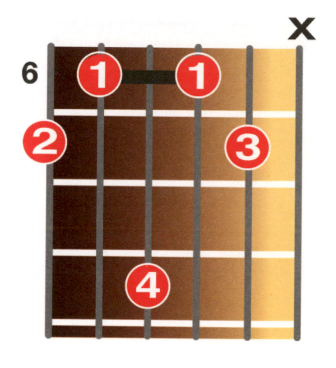

Chord Spelling
1st (B), 3rd (D#), 5th (F#), 9th (C#)

Bm9
B Minor 9th
(1st position)

A
B♭/A♯
B
C
C♯/D♭
D
E♭/D♯
E
F
F♯/G♭
G
A♭/G♯
Other Chords

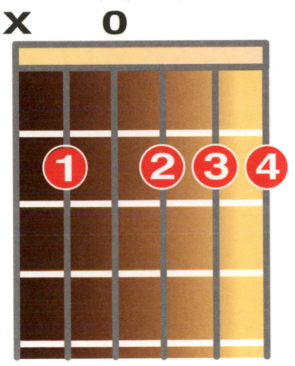

Chord Spelling
1st (B), ♭3rd (D), 5th (F♯), ♭7th (A), 9th (C♯)

Bmaj9
B Major 9th

(1st position)

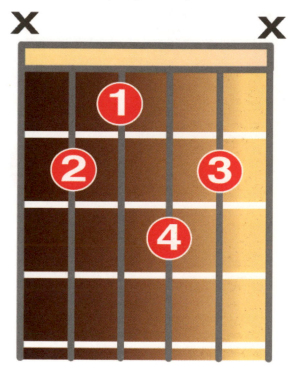

Chord Spelling

1st (B), 3rd (D#), 5th (F#), 7th (A#), 9th (C#)

A
B♭/A#
B
C
C#/D♭
D
E♭/D#
E
F
F#/G♭
G
A♭/G#
Other Chords

B+

B Augmented

(1st position)

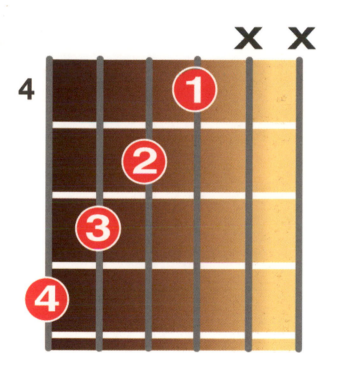

Chord Spelling

1st (B), 3rd (D♯), ♯5th (Fx)

A

B♭/A♯

B

C

C♯/D♭

D

E♭/D♯

E

F

F♯/G♭

G

A♭/G♯

Other Chords

A

B♭/A#

B

C

C#/D♭

D

E♭/D#

E

F

F#/G♭

G

A♭/G#

Other Chords

B⁰⁷

B Diminished 7th

(1st position)

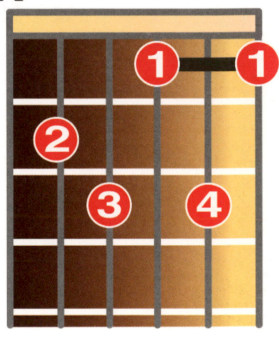

Chord Spelling

1st (B), ♭3rd (D), ♭5th (F), ♭♭7th (A♭)

B⁰

B Diminished triad

(1st position)

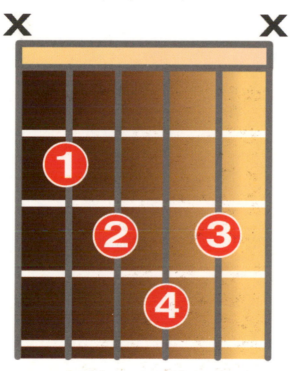

A

B♭/A♯

B

C

C♯/D♭

D

E♭/D♯

E

F

F♯/G♭

G

A♭/G♯

Other Chords

Chord Spelling

1st (B), ♭3rd (D), ♭5th (F)

C
C Major
(1st position)

A
Bb/A#
B
C
C#/Db
D
Eb/D#
E
F
F#/Gb
G
Ab/G#
Other Chords

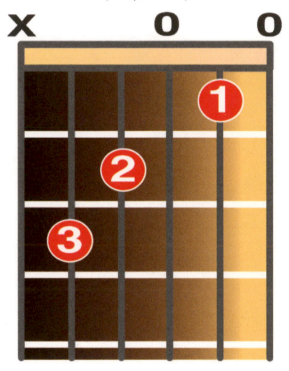

Chord Spelling

1st (C), 3rd (E), 5th (G)

C
C Major
(2nd position)

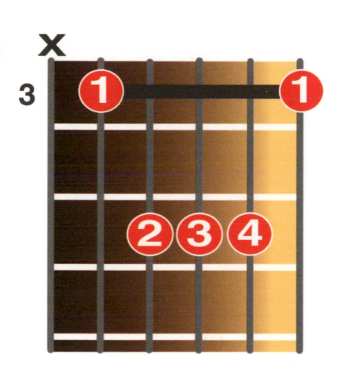

Chord Spelling

1st (C), 3rd (E), 5th (G)

A

B♭/A♯

B

C

C♯/D♭

D

E♭/D♯

E

F

F♯/G♭

G

A♭/G♯

Other Chords

Cm
C Minor
(1st position)

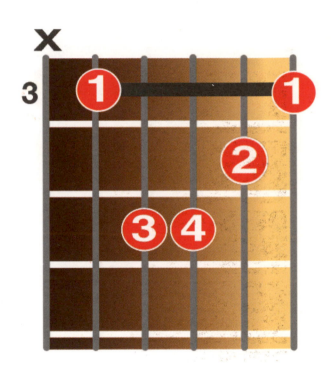

A
B♭/A♯
B
C
C♯/D♭
D
E♭/D♯
E
F
F♯/G♭
G
A♭/G♯
Other Chords

X

3

1   1

2

3   4

Chord Spelling
1st (C), ♭3rd (E♭), 5th (G)

Cm
C Minor
(2nd position)

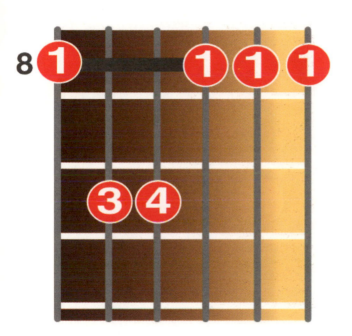

8

A

B♭/A♯

B

C

C♯/D♭

D

E♭/D♯

E

F

F♯/G♭

G

A♭/G♯

Other Chords

Chord Spelling

1st (C), ♭3rd (E♭), 5th (G)

Cmaj7
C Major 7th

(1st position)

A

B♭/A♯

B

C

C♯/D♭

D

E♭/D♯

E

F

F♯/G♭

G

A♭/G♯

Other Chords

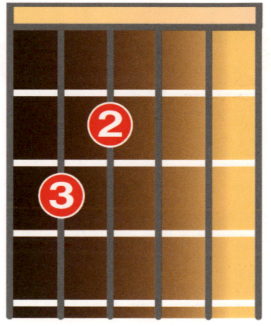

Chord Spelling

1st (C), 3rd (E), 5th (G), 7th (B)

Cmaj7
C Major 7th
(2nd position)

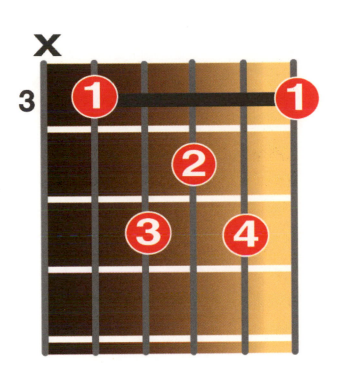

A
B♭/A♯
B
C
C♯/D♭
D
E♭/D♯
E
F
F♯/G♭
G
A♭/G♯
Other Chords

Chord Spelling
1st (C), 3rd (E), 5th (G), 7th (B)

Cm7
C Minor 7th
(1st position)

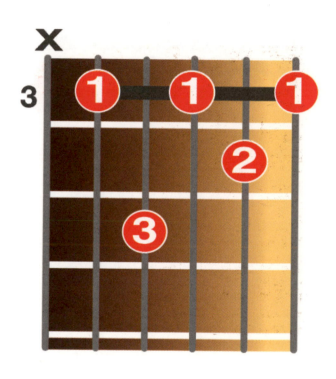

Chord Spelling
1st (C), ♭3rd (E♭), 5th (G), ♭7th (B♭)

Cm7
C Minor 7th
(2nd position)

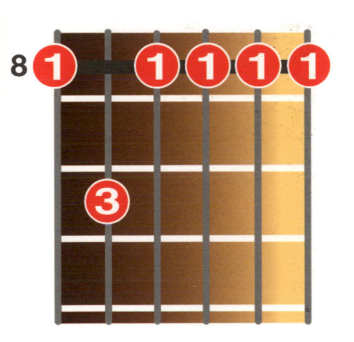

A
B♭/A♯
B
C
C♯/D♭
D
E♭/D♯
E
F
F♯/G♭
G
A♭/G♯
Other Chords

8

Chord Spelling
1st (C), ♭3rd (E♭), 5th (G), ♭7th (B♭)

A
B♭/A♯
B
C
C♯/D♭
D
E♭/D♯
E
F
F♯/G♭
G
A♭/G♯
Other Chords

Csus4
C Suspended 4th

(1st position)

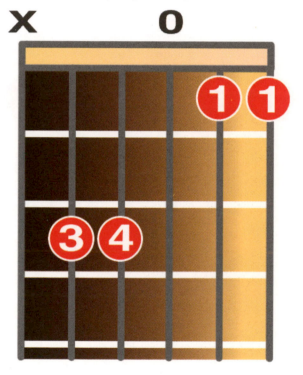

Chord Spelling

1st (C), 4th (F), 5th (G)

Csus4
C Suspended 4th
(2nd position)

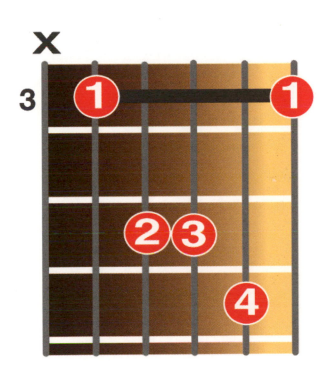

Chord Spelling
1st (C), 4th (F), 5th (G)

A
B♭/A♯
B
C
C♯/D♭
D
E♭/D♯
E
F
F♯/G♭
G
A♭/G♯
Other Chords

C7sus4
C Dominant 7th sus4
(1st position)

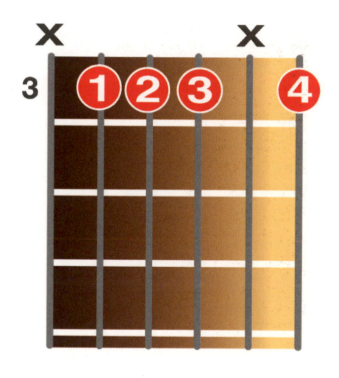

Chord Spelling
1st (C), 4th (F), 5th (G), ♭7th (B♭)

C7sus4
C Dominant 7th sus4

(2nd position)

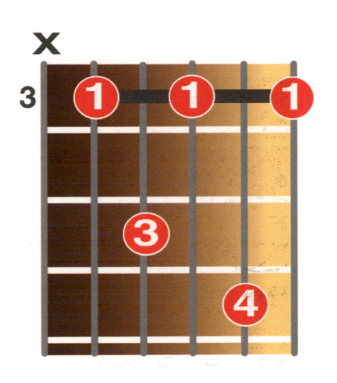

Chord Spelling

1st (C), 4th (F), 5th (G), ♭7th (B♭)

A
B♭/A#
B
C
C#/D♭
D
E♭/D#
E
F
F#/G♭
G
A♭/G#
Other Chords

C6
C Major 6th
(1st position)

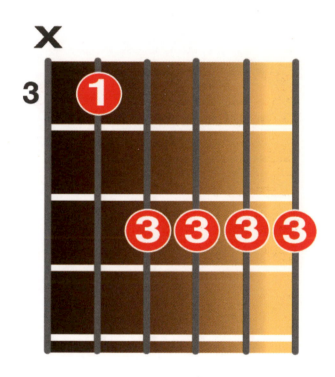

Chord Spelling
1st (C), 3rd (E), 5th (G), 6th (A)

A
Bb/A#
B
C
C#/Db
D
Eb/D#
E
F
F#/Gb
G
Ab/G#
Other Chords

C6
C Major 6th
(2nd position)

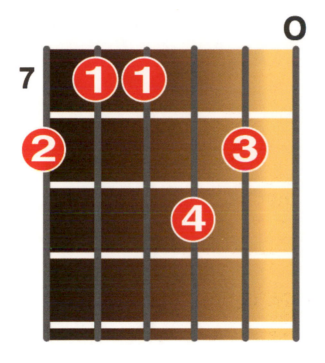

7

O

A
Bb/A#
B
C
C#/Db
D
Eb/D#
E
F
F#/Gb
G
Ab/G#
Other Chords

Chord Spelling
1st (C), 3rd (E), 5th (G), 6th (A)

Cm6
C Minor 6th
(1st position)

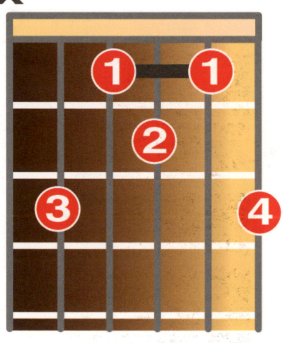

Chord Spelling
1st (C), ♭3rd (E♭), 5th (G), 6th (A)

Cm6
C Minor 6th
(2nd position)

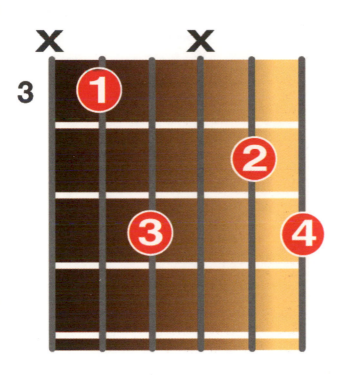

A

B♭/A♯

B

C

C♯/D♭

D

E♭/D♯

E

F

F♯/G♭

G

A♭/G♯

Other
Chords

Chord Spelling

1st (C), ♭3rd (E♭), 5th (G), 6th (A)

A
B♭/A♯
B
C
C♯/D♭
D
E♭/D♯
E
F
F♯/G♭
G
A♭/G♯
Other Chords

C7

C Dominant 7th

(1st position)

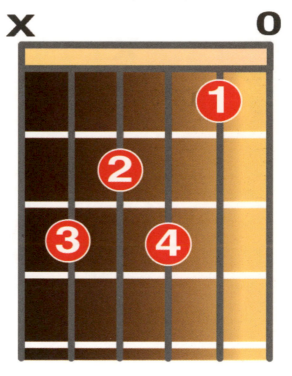

Chord Spelling

1st (C), 3rd (E), 5th (G), ♭7th (B♭)

C7
C Dominant 7th
(2nd position)

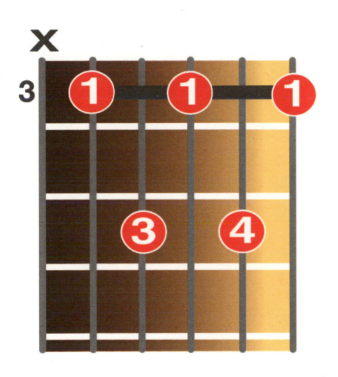

A

B♭/A♯

B

C

C♯/D♭

D

E♭/D♯

E

F

F♯/G♭

G

A♭/G♯

Other Chords

Chord Spelling

1st (C), 3rd (E), 5th (G), ♭7th (B♭)

C9

C Dominant 9th

(1st position)

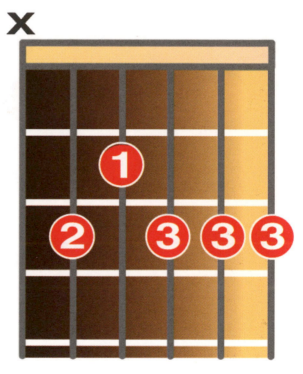

Chord Spelling

1st (C), 3rd (E), 5th (G), ♭7th (B♭), 9th (D)

A
B♭/A♯
B
C
C♯/D♭
D
E♭/D♯
E
F
F♯/G♭
G
A♭/G♯
Other Chords

C9

C Dominant 9th

(2nd position)

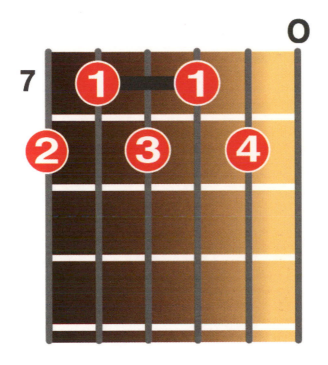

A

B♭/A♯

B

C

C♯/D♭

D

E♭/D♯

E

F

F♯/G♭

G

A♭/G♯

Other Chords

Chord Spelling

1st (C), 3rd (E), 5th (G), ♭7th (B♭), 9th (D)

C5

C 5th 'power chord'

(1st position)

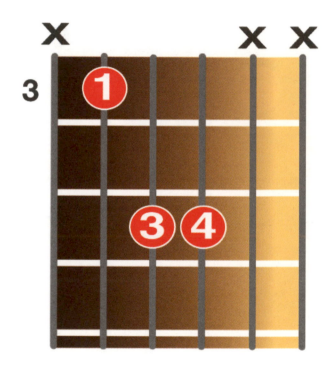

Chord Spelling

1st (C), 5th (G)

C^6_9
C Major 6th add 9th

(1st position)

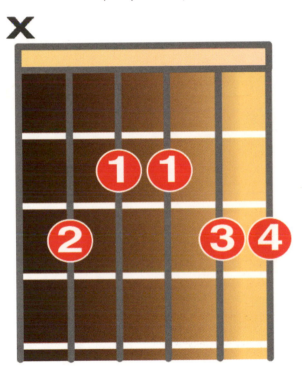

Chord Spelling

1st (C), 3rd (E), 5th (G), 6th (A), 9th (D)

A
B♭/A♯
B
C
C♯/D♭
D
E♭/D♯
E
F
F♯/G♭
G
A♭/G♯
Other Chords

C11
C Dominant 11th
(1st position)

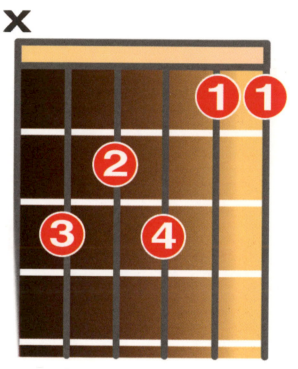

Chord Spelling
1st (C), 3rd (E), 5th (G), ♭7th (B♭), 9th (D), 11th (F)

C13
C Dominant 13th
(1st position)

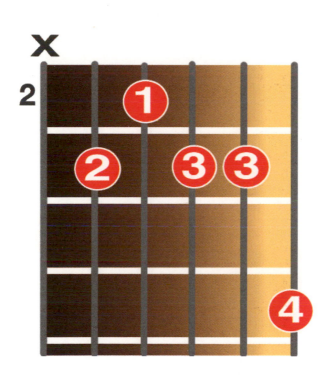

A
B♭/A♯
B
C
C♯/D♭
D
E♭/D♯
E
F
F♯/G♭
G
A♭/G♯
Other Chords

Chord Spelling
1st (C), 3rd (E), 5th (G), ♭7th (B♭), 9th (D), 13th (A)

Cadd9
C Major add 9th
(1st position)

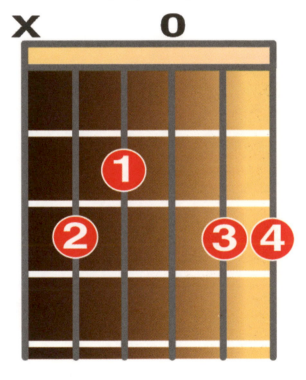

Chord Spelling
1st (C), 3rd (E), 5th (G), 9th (D)

Cm9
C Minor 9th
(1st position)

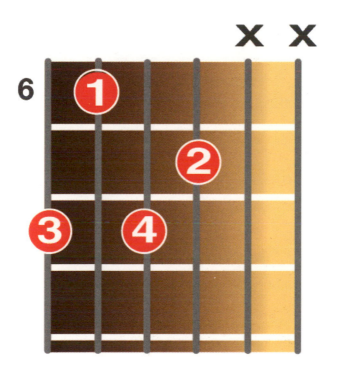

A

B♭/A♯

B

C

C♯/D♭

D

E♭/D♯

E

F

F♯/G♭

G

A♭/G♯

Other
Chords

Chord Spelling

1st (C), ♭3rd (E♭), 5th (G), ♭7th (B♭), 9th (D)

Cmaj9
C Major 9th
(1st position)

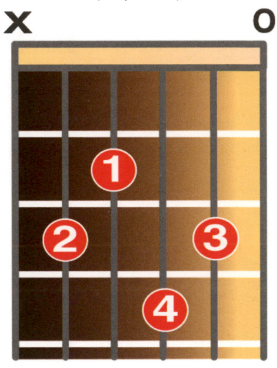

Chord Spelling
1st (C), 3rd (E), 5th (G), 7th (B), 9th (D)

C+
C Augmented
(1st position)

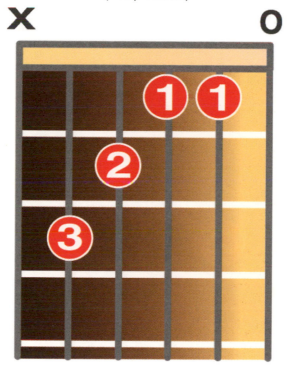

X   O

Chord Spelling

1st (C), 3rd (E), #5th (G#)

A

B♭/A♯

B

C

C♯/D♭

D

E♭/D♯

E

F

F♯/G♭

G

A♭/G♯

Other
Chords

C⁰⁷

C Diminished 7th

(1st position)

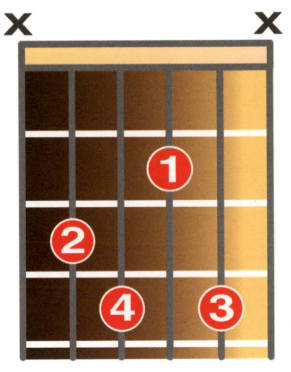

Chord Spelling

1st (C), ♭3rd (E♭), ♭5th (G♭), ♭♭7th (B♭♭)

A
B♭/A♯
B
C
C♯/D♭
D
E♭/D♯
E
F
F♯/G♭
G
A♭/G♯
Other Chords

C⁰

C Diminished triad

(1st position)

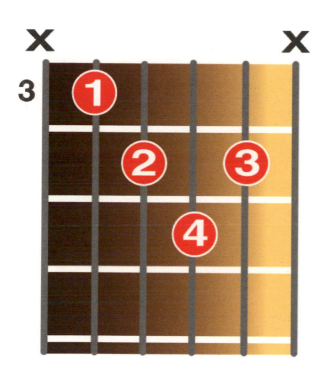

Chord Spelling

1st (C), ♭3rd (E♭), ♭5th (G♭)

C#

C# Major

(1st position)

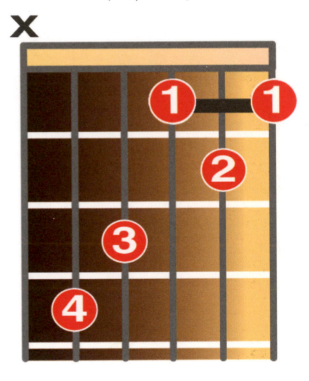

Chord Spelling

1st (C#), 3rd (E#), 5th (G#)

A
Bb/A#
B
C
C#/Db
D
Eb/D#
E
F
F#/Gb
G
Ab/G#
Other Chords

C♯

C♯ Major

(2nd position)

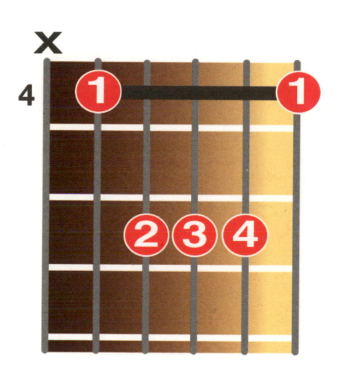

A

B♭/A♯

B

C

C♯/D♭

D

E♭/D♯

E

F

F♯/G♭

G

A♭/G♯

Other Chords

Chord Spelling

1st (C♯), 3rd (E♯), 5th (G♯)

C#m
C# Minor

(1st position)

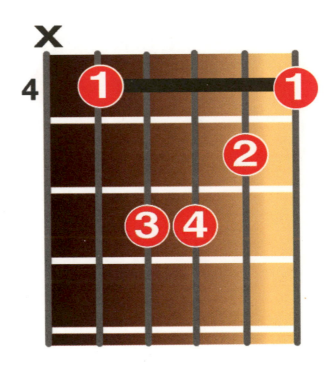

Chord Spelling

1st (C#), ♭3rd (E), 5th (G#)

C#m
C# Minor
(2nd position)

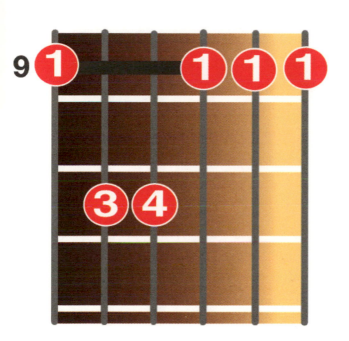

A
Bb/A#
B
C
C#/Db
D
Eb/D#
E
F
F#/Gb
G
Ab/G#
Other Chords

Chord Spelling
1st (C#), b3rd (E), 5th (G#)

C#maj7
C# Major 7th

(1st position)

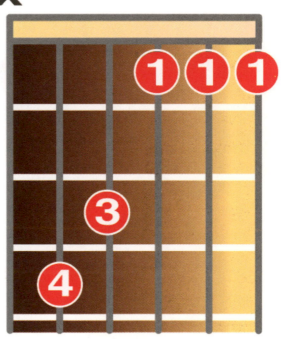

A
B♭/A♯
B
C
C♯/D♭
D
E♭/D♯
E
F
F♯/G♭
G
A♭/G♯
Other Chords

Chord Spelling

1st (C#), 3rd (E#), 5th (G#), 7th (B#)

C#maj7
C# Major 7th
(2nd position)

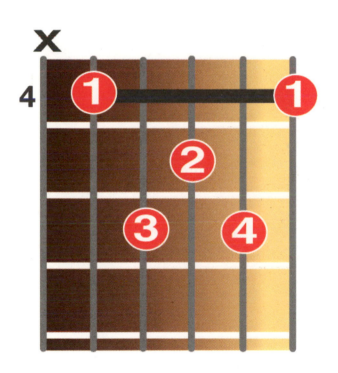

A
Bb/A#
B
C
C#/Db
D
Eb/D#
E
F
F#/Gb
G
Ab/G#
Other Chords

Chord Spelling

1st (C#), 3rd (E#), 5th (G#), 7th (B#)

C#m7
C# Minor 7th
(1st position)

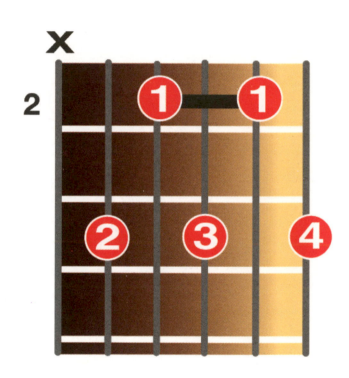

Chord Spelling
1st (C#), ♭3rd (E), 5th (G#), ♭7th (B)

C#m7
C# Minor 7th
(2nd position)

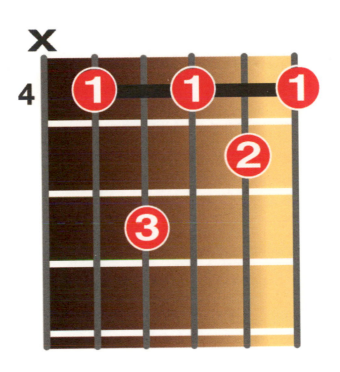

Chord Spelling

1st (C#), b3rd (E), 5th (G#), b7th (B)

A

Bb/A#

B

C

C#/Db

D

Eb/D#

E

F

F#/Gb

G

Ab/G#

Other
Chords

C#sus4
C# Suspended 4th

(1st position)

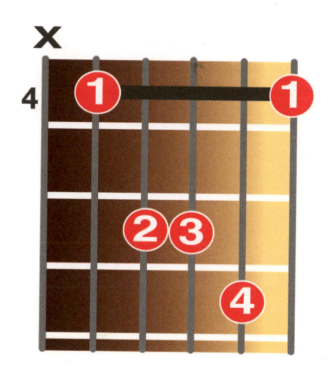

Chord Spelling

1st (C#), 4th (F#), 5th (G#)

C#sus4
C# Suspended 4th
(2nd position)

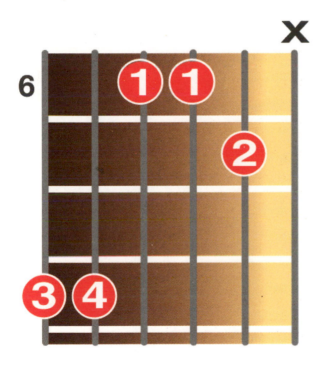

Chord Spelling

1st (C#), 4th (F#), 5th (G#)

A

B♭/A#

B

C

C#/D♭

D

E♭/D#

E

F

F#/G♭

G

A♭/G#

Other Chords

C#7sus4
C# Dominant 7th sus4
(1st position)

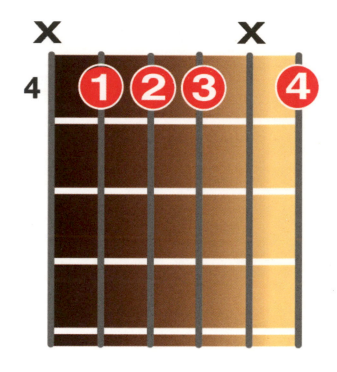

Chord Spelling
1st (C#), 4th (F#), 5th (G#), ♭7th (B)

C♯7sus4
C♯ Dominant 7th sus4
(2nd position)

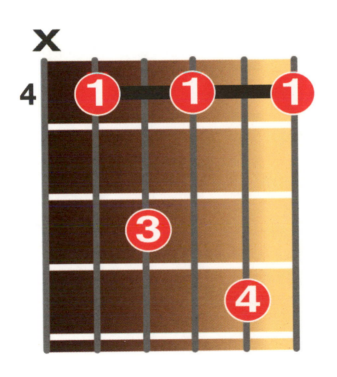

Chord Spelling
1st (C♯), 4th (F♯), 5th (G♯), ♭7th (B)

A

B♭/A♯

B

C

C♯/D♭

D

E♭/D♯

E

F

F♯/G♭

G

A♭/G♯

Other Chords

C#6
C# Major 6th
(1st position)

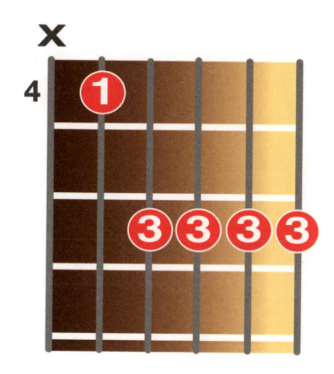

Chord Spelling
1st (C#), 3rd (E#), 5th (G#), 6th (A#)

C#6
C# Major 6th
(2nd position)

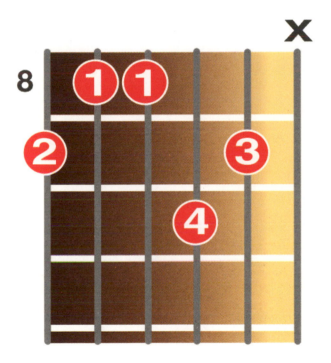

8

X

A

B♭/A#

B

C

C#/D♭

D

E♭/D#

E

F

F#/G♭

G

A♭/G#

Other Chords

Chord Spelling
1st (C#), 3rd (E#), 5th (G#), 6th (A#)

C#m6
C# Minor 6th
(1st position)

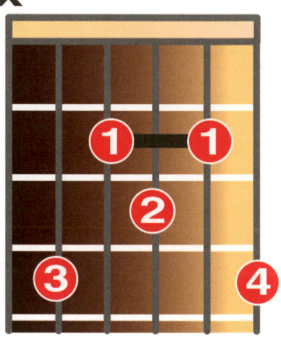

Chord Spelling
1st (C#), ♭3rd (E), 5th (G#), 6th (A#)

A
B♭/A#
B
C
C#/D♭
D
E♭/D#
E
F
F#/G♭
G
A♭/G#
Other Chords

C#m6
C# Minor 6th

(2nd position)

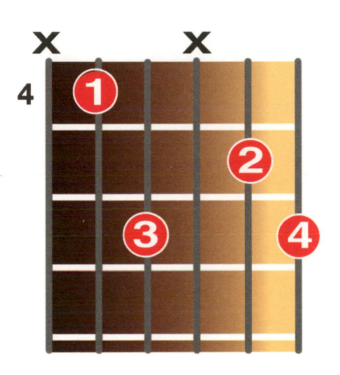

A
Bb/A#
B
C
C#/Db
D
Eb/D#
E
F
F#/Gb
G
Ab/G#
Other Chords

Chord Spelling

1st (C#), b3rd (E), 5th (G#), 6th (A#)

C#7

C# Dominant 7th

(1st position)

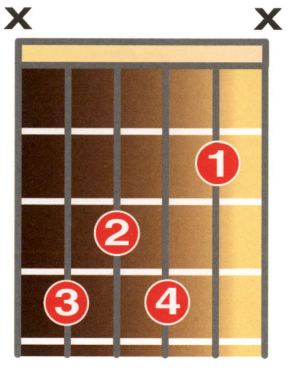

Chord Spelling

1st (C#), 3rd (E#), 5th (G#), ♭7th (B)

C#7

C# Dominant 7th

(2nd position)

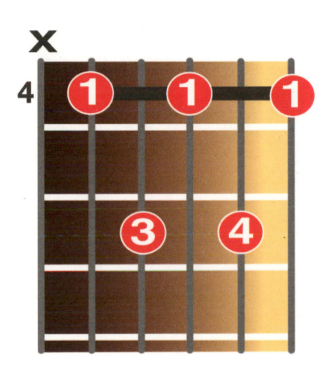

A

B♭/A♯

B

C

C♯/D♭

D

E♭/D♯

E

F

F♯/G♭

G

A♭/G♯

Other Chords

Chord Spelling

1st (C#), 3rd (E#), 5th (G#), ♭7th (B)

C#9

C# Dominant 9th

(1st position)

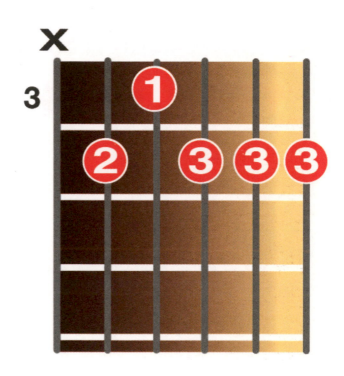

Chord Spelling

1st (C#), 3rd (E#), 5th (G#), ♭7th (B), 9th (D#)

C#9

C# Dominant 9th

(2nd position)

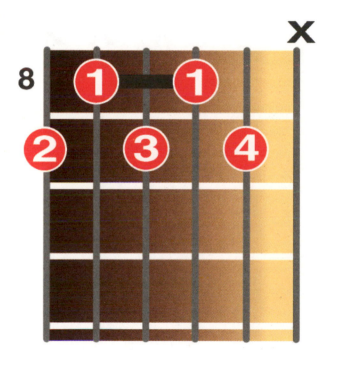

8

X

Chord Spelling

1st (C#), 3rd (E#), 5th (G#), ♭7th (B), 9th (D#)

A
B♭/A#
B
C
C#/D♭
D
E♭/D#
E
F
F#/G♭
G
A♭/G#
Other Chords

C♯5

C♯ 5th 'power chord'

(1st position)

A
B♭/A♯
B
C
C♯/D♭
D
E♭/D♯
E
F
F♯/G♭
G
A♭/G♯
Other Chords

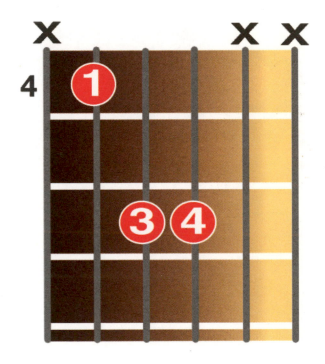

Chord Spelling

1st (C♯), 5th (G♯)

C#⁶₉

C# Major 6th add 9th

(1st position)

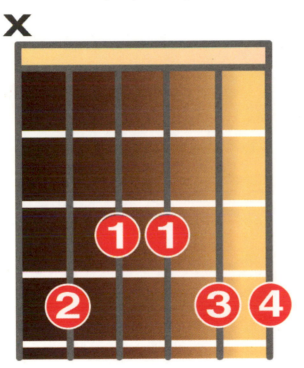

Chord Spelling

1st (C#), 3rd (E#), 5th (G#), 6th (A#), 9th (D#)

A

B♭/A#

B

C

C#/D♭

D

E♭/D#

E

F

F#/G♭

G

A♭/G#

Other Chords

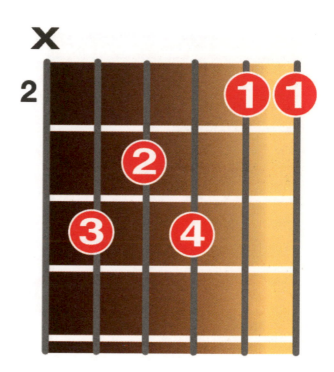

C#11
C# Dominant 11th
(1st position)

A

B♭/A♯

B

C

C♯/D♭

D

E♭/D♯

E

F

F♯/G♭

G

A♭/G♯

Other Chords

Chord Spelling
1st (C♯), 3rd (E♯), 5th (G♯), ♭7th (B), 9th (D♯), 11th (F♯)

C♯13
C♯ Dominant 13th
(1st position)

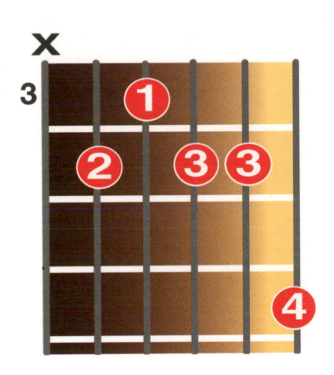

A

B♭/A♯

B

C

C♯/D♭

D

E♭/D♯

E

F

F♯/G♭

G

A♭/G♯

Other Chords

Chord Spelling

st (C♯), 3rd (E♯), 5th (G♯), ♭7th (B), 9th (D♯), 13th (A♯)

C#add9
C# Major add 9th
(1st position)

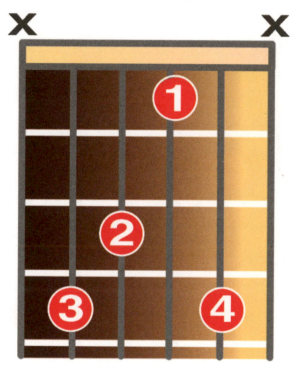

A
Bb/A#
B
C
C#/Db
D
Eb/D#
E
F
F#/Gb
G
Ab/G#
Other Chords

Chord Spelling
1st (C#), 3rd (E#), 5th (G#), 9th (D#)

C#m9
C# Minor 9th
(1st position)

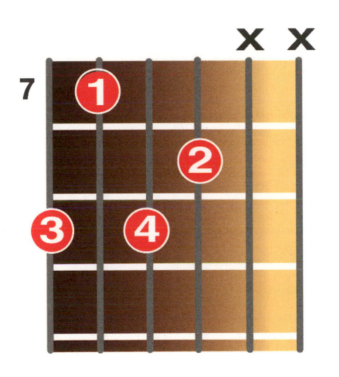

A
B♭/A♯
B
C
C♯/D♭
D
E♭/D♯
E
F
F♯/G♭
G
A♭/G♯
Other Chords

Chord Spelling
1st (C#), ♭3rd (E), 5th (G#), ♭7th (B), 9th (D#)

C#maj9
C# Major 9th

(1st position)

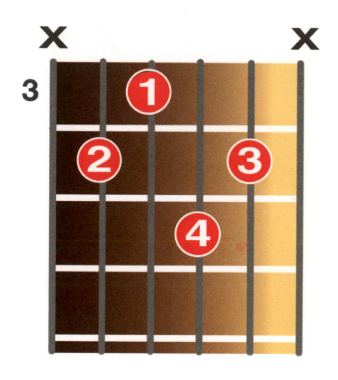

Chord Spelling

1st (C#), 3rd (E#), 5th (G#), 7th (B#), 9th (D#)

C♯+
C♯ Augmented
(1st position)

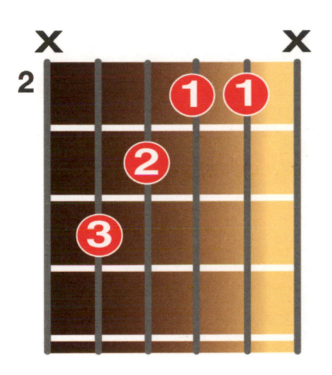

A
B♭/A♯
B
C
C♯/D♭
D
E♭/D♯
E
F
F♯/G♭
G
A♭/G♯
Other Chords

Chord Spelling

1st (C♯), 3rd (E♯), ♯5th (Gx)

C#⁰⁷

C# Diminished 7th

(1st position)

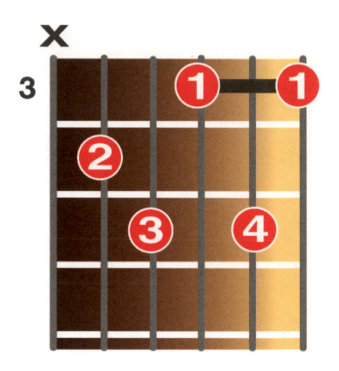

Chord Spelling

1st (C#), ♭3rd (E), ♭5th (G), ♭♭7th (B♭)

C#⁰

C# Diminished triad

(1st position)

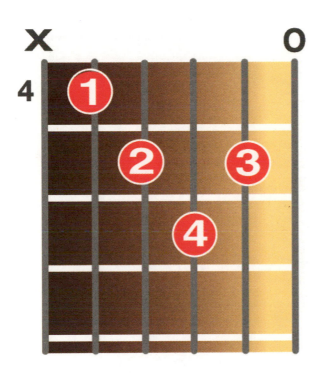

A

B♭/A♯

B

C

C♯/D♭

D

E♭/D♯

E

F

F♯/G♭

G

A♭/G♯

Other Chords

Chord Spelling

1st (C#), ♭3rd (E), ♭5th (G)

D

D Major

(1st position)

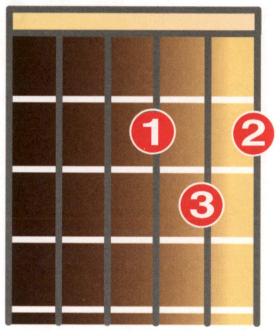

Chord Spelling

1st (D), 3rd (F#), 5th (A)

D
D Major
(2nd position)

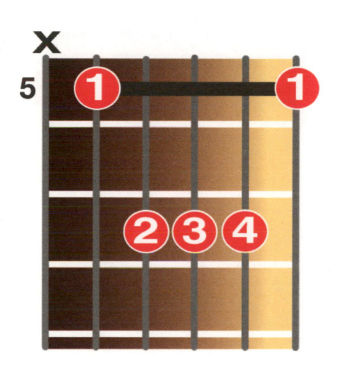

X

5

Chord Spelling

1st (D), 3rd (F♯), 5th (A)

A
B♭/A♯
B
C
C♯/D♭
D
E♭/D♯
E
F
F♯/G♭
G
A♭/G♯
Other Chords

Dm
D Minor
(1st position)

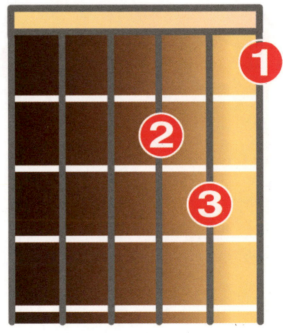

Chord Spelling

1st (D), ♭3rd (F), 5th (A)

Dm
D Minor
(2nd position)

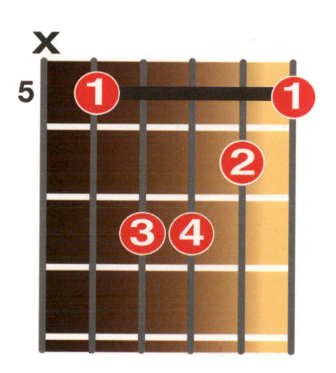

Chord Spelling

1st (D), ♭3rd (F), 5th (A)

A

B♭/A#

B

C

C#/D♭

D

E♭/D#

E

F

F#/G♭

G

A♭/G#

Other Chords

Dmaj7
D Major 7th
(1st position)

A
B♭/A♯
B
C
C♯/D♭
D
E♭/D♯
E
F
F♯/G♭
G
A♭/G♯
Other Chords

X X O

Chord Spelling
1st (D), 3rd (F♯), 5th (A), 7th (C♯)

Dmaj7
D Major 7th
(2nd position)

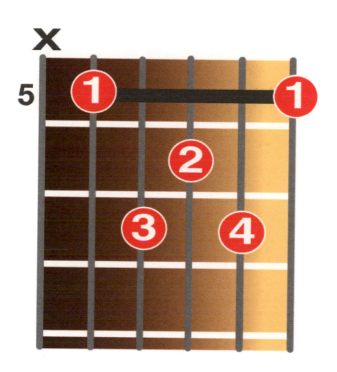

A
Bb/A#
B
C
C#/Db
D
Eb/D#
E
F
F#/Gb
G
Ab/G#
Other Chords

Chord Spelling
1st (D), 3rd (F#), 5th (A), 7th (C#)

Dm7
D Minor 7th
(1st position)

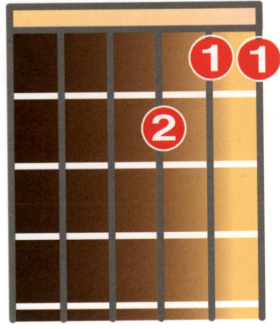

Chord Spelling

1st (D), ♭3rd (F), 5th (A), ♭7th (C)

Dm7
D Minor 7th
(2nd position)

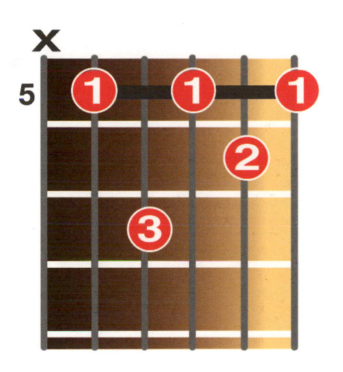

A
B♭/A♯
B
C
C♯/D♭
D
E♭/D♯
E
F
F♯/G♭
G
A♭/G♯
Other Chords

Chord Spelling

1st (D), ♭3rd (F), 5th (A), ♭7th (C)

A

B♭/A♯

B

C

C♯/D♭

D

E♭/D♯

E

F

F♯/G♭

G

A♭/G♯

Other Chords

Dsus4
D Suspended 4th

(1st position)

X X O

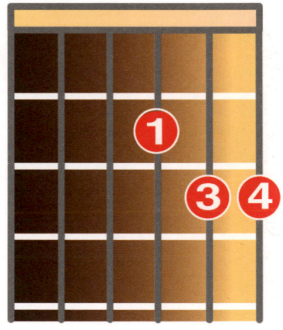

Chord Spelling

1st (D), 4th (G), 5th (A)

Dsus4
D Suspended 4th
(2nd position)

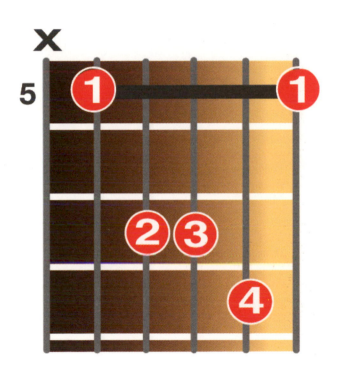

Chord Spelling

1st (D), 4th (G), 5th (A)

A
Bb/A#
B
C
C#/Db
D
Eb/D#
E
F
F#/Gb
G
Ab/G#
Other Chords

D7sus4
D Dominant 7th sus4
(1st position)

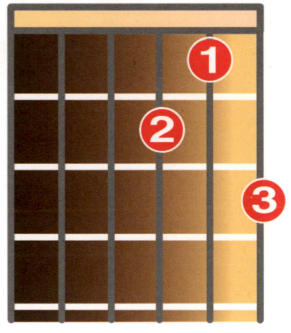

Chord Spelling
1st (D), 4th (G), 5th (A), ♭7th (C)

D7sus4
D Dominant 7th sus4

(2nd position)

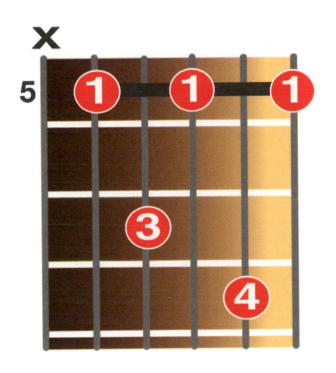

Chord Spelling

1st (D), 4th (G), 5th (A), ♭7th (C)

A

B♭/A♯

B

C

C♯/D♭

D

E♭/D♯

E

F

F♯/G♭

G

A♭/G♯

Other Chords

D6
D Major 6th
(1st position)

X X O O

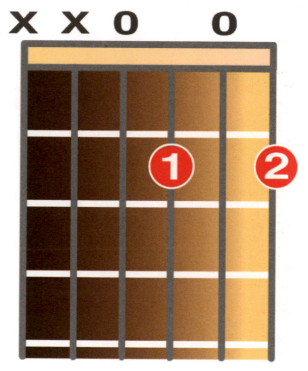

Chord Spelling
1st (D), 3rd (F♯), 5th (A), 6th (B)

A
B♭/A♯
B
C
C♯/D♭
D
E♭/D♯
E
F
F♯/G♭
G
A♭/G♯
Other Chords

D6
D Major 6th
(2nd position)

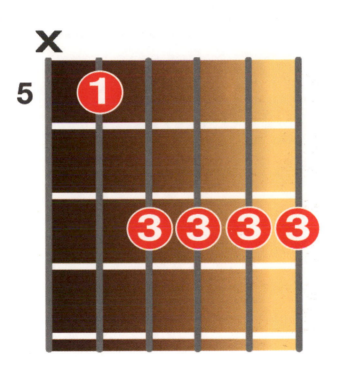

A
B♭/A♯
B
C
C♯/D♭
D
E♭/D♯
E
F
F♯/G♭
G
A♭/G♯
Other Chords

Chord Spelling

1st (D), 3rd (F♯), 5th (A), 6th (B)

Dm6
D Minor 6th
(1st position)

X X O

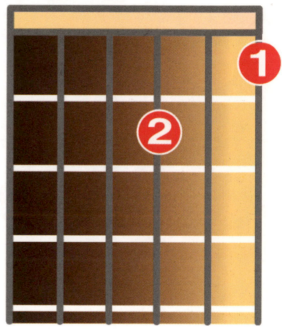

Chord Spelling
1st (D), ♭3rd (F), 5th (A), 6th (B)

A
B♭/A♯
B
C
C♯/D♭
D
E♭/D♯
E
F
F♯/G♭
G
A♭/G♯
Other Chords

Dm6
D Minor 6th
(2nd position)

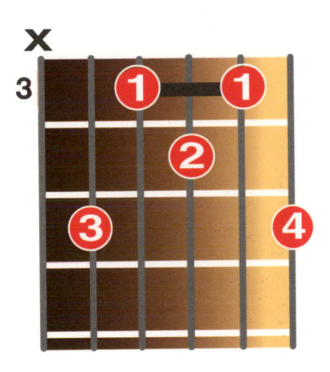

Chord Spelling
1st (D), ♭3rd (F), 5th (A), 6th (B)

A
B♭/A♯
B
C
C♯/D♭
D
E♭/D♯
E
F
F♯/G♭
G
A♭/G♯
Other Chords

A
B♭/A♯
B
C
C♯/D♭
D
E♭/D♯
E
F
F♯/G♭
G
A♭/G♯
Other Chords

D7
D Dominant 7th

(1st position)

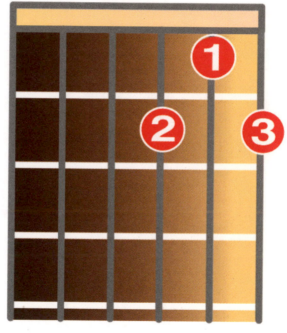

Chord Spelling

1st (D), 3rd (F♯), 5th (A), ♭7th (C)

D7

D Dominant 7th

(2nd position)

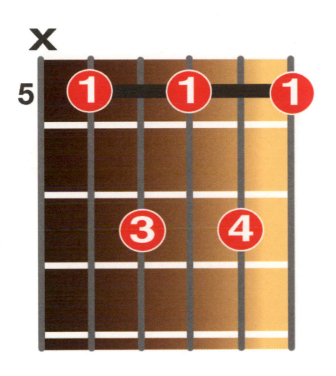

Chord Spelling

1st (D), 3rd (F♯), 5th (A), ♭7th (C)

A

B♭/A♯

B

C

C♯/D♭

D

E♭/D♯

E

F

F♯/G♭

G

A♭/G♯

Other Chords

D9
D Dominant 9th
(1st position)

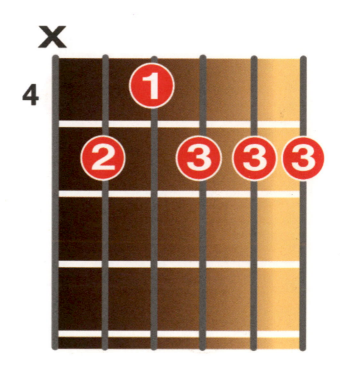

Chord Spelling
1st (D), 3rd (F♯), 5th (A), ♭7th (C), 9th (E)

A
B♭/A♯
B
C
C♯/D♭
D
E♭/D♯
E
F
F♯/G♭
G
A♭/G♯
Other Chords

D9
D Dominant 9th
(2nd position)

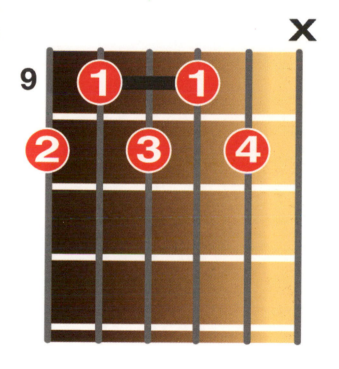

A
Bb/A#
B
C
C#/Db
D
Eb/D#
E
F
F#/Gb
G
Ab/G#
Other Chords

Chord Spelling
1st (D), 3rd (F#), 5th (A), b7th (C), 9th (E)

D5

D 5th 'power chord'

(1st position)

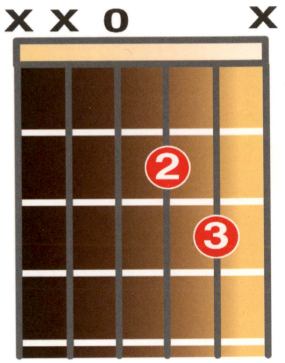

Chord Spelling

1st (D), 5th (A)

D⁶₉

D Major 6th add 9th

(1st position)

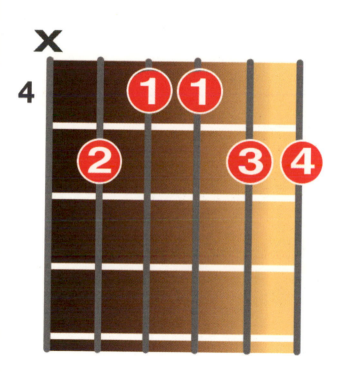

Chord Spelling

1st (D), 3rd (F♯), 5th (A), 6th (B), 9th (E)

A
B♭/A♯
B
C
C♯/D♭
D
E♭/D♯
E
F
F♯/G♭
G
A♭/G♯
Other Chords

D11
D Dominant 11th
(1st position)

A
B♭/A♯
B
C
C♯/D♭
D
E♭/D♯
E
F
F♯/G♭
G
A♭/G♯
Other Chords

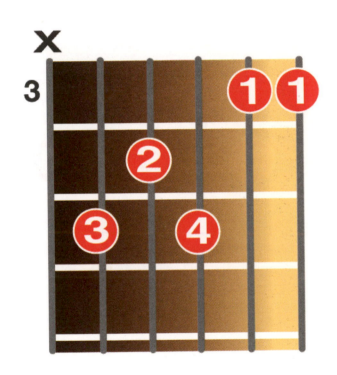

Chord Spelling

1st (D), 3rd (F♯), 5th (A), ♭7th (C), 9th (E), 11th (G

D13

D Dominant 13th

(1st position)

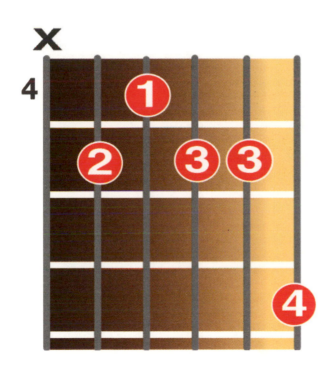

A

B♭/A♯

B

C

C♯/D♭

D

E♭/D♯

E

F

F♯/G♭

G

A♭/G♯

Other Chords

Chord Spelling

1st (D), 3rd (F♯), 5th (A), ♭7th (C), 9th (E), 13th (B)

Dadd9
D Major add 9th
(1st position)

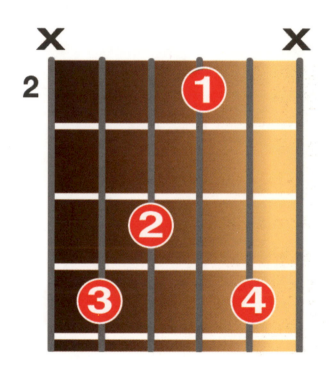

Chord Spelling
1st (D), 3rd (F#), 5th (A), 9th (E)

A
B♭/A#
B
C
C#/D♭
D
E♭/D#
E
F
F#/G♭
G
A♭/G#
Other Chords

Dm9
D Minor 9th
(1st position)

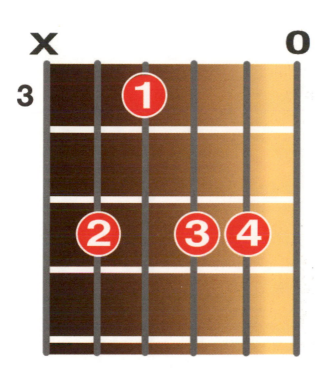

X   O

3

A

B♭/A♯

B

C

C♯/D♭

D

E♭/D♯

E

F

F♯/G♭

G

A♭/G♯

Other Chords

Chord Spelling
1st (D), ♭3rd (F), 5th (A), ♭7th (C), 9th (E)

Dmaj9
D Major 9th
(1st position)

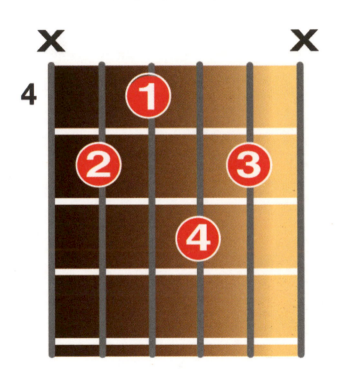

Chord Spelling
1st (D), 3rd (F#), 5th (A), 7th (C#), 9th (E)

A
B♭/A#
B
C
C#/D♭
D
E♭/D#
E
F
F#/G♭
G
A♭/G#
Other Chords

D+

D Augmented

(1st position)

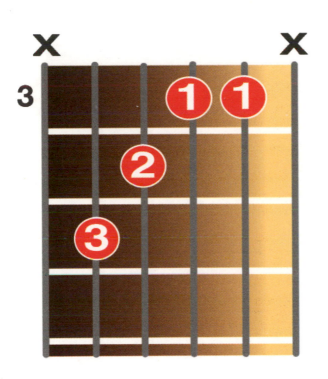

A

Bb/A#

B

C

C#/Db

D

Eb/D#

E

F

F#/Gb

G

Ab/G#

Other Chords

Chord Spelling

1st (D), 3rd (F#), #5th (A#)

D⁰⁷

D Diminished 7th

(1st position)

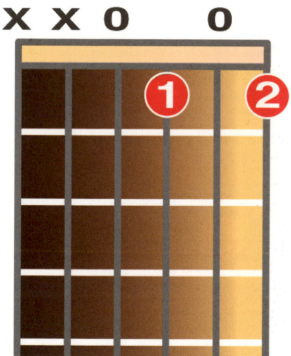

Chord Spelling

1st (D), ♭3rd (F), ♭5th (A♭), ♭♭7th (C♭)

D⁰

D Diminished triad

(1st position)

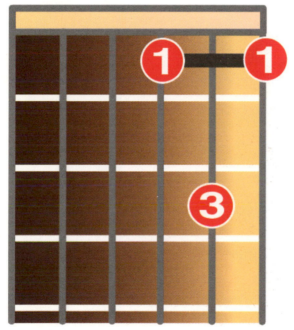

Chord Spelling

1st (D), ♭3rd (F), ♭5th (A♭)

A

B♭/A♯

B

C

C♯/D♭

D

E♭/D♯

E

F

F♯/G♭

G

A♭/G♯

Other Chords

E♭

E♭ Major

(1st position)

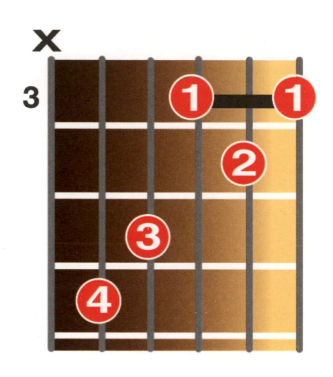

Chord Spelling
1st (E♭), 3rd (G), 5th (B♭)

A
B♭/A#
B
C
C#/D♭
D
E♭/D#
E
F
F#/G♭
G
A♭/G#
Other Chords

E♭

E♭ Major

(2nd position)

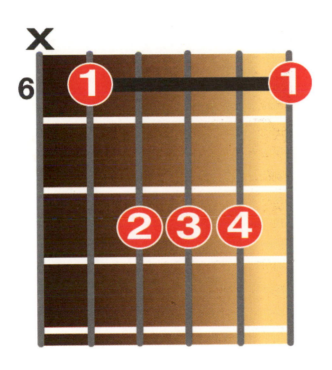

X

6

1   1

2   3   4

A

B♭/A♯

B

C

C♯/D♭

D

E♭/D♯

E

F

F♯/G♭

G

A♭/G♯

Other Chords

Chord Spelling

1st (E♭), 3rd (G), 5th (B♭)

E♭m
E♭ Minor
(1st position)

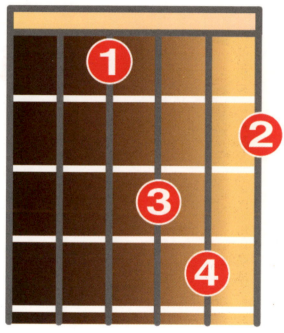

Chord Spelling
1st (E♭), ♭3rd (G♭), 5th (B♭)

E♭m
E♭ Minor
(2nd position)

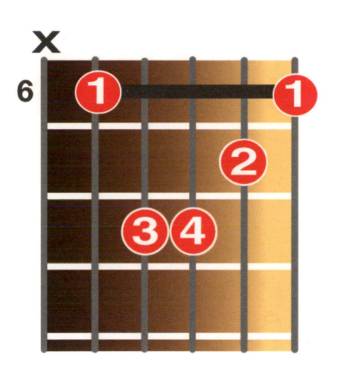

Chord Spelling

1st (E♭), ♭3rd (G♭), 5th (B♭)

A
B♭/A#
B
C
C#/D♭
D
E♭/D#
E
F
F#/G♭
G
A♭/G#
Other Chords

E♭maj7
E♭ Major 7th

(1st position)

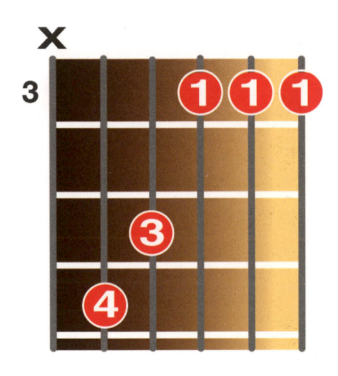

Chord Spelling

1st (E♭), 3rd (G), 5th (B♭), 7th (D)

A

B♭/A#

B

C

C#/D♭

D

E♭/D#

E

F

F#/G♭

G

A♭/G#

Other Chords

E♭maj7
E♭ Major 7th
(2nd position)

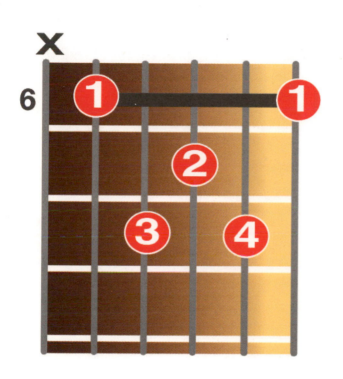

Chord Spelling

1st (E♭), 3rd (G), 5th (B♭), 7th (D)

A

B♭/A#

B

C

C#/D♭

D

E♭/D#

E

F

F#/G♭

G

A♭/G#

Other Chords

E♭m7
E♭ Minor 7th

(1st position)

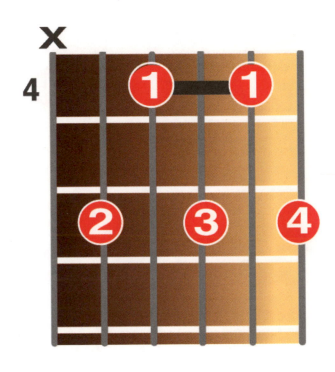

Chord Spelling

1st (E♭), ♭3rd (G♭), 5th (B♭), ♭7th (D♭)

A
B♭/A♯
B
C
C♯/D♭
D
E♭/D♯
E
F
F♯/G♭
G
A♭/G♯
Other Chords

E♭m7
E♭ Minor 7th

(2nd position)

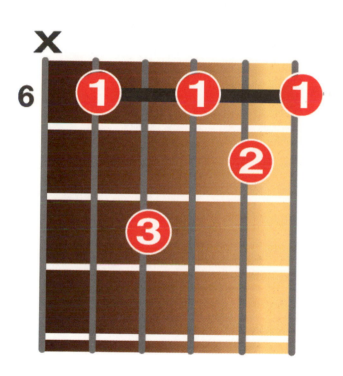

Chord Spelling

1st (E♭), ♭3rd (G♭), 5th (B♭), ♭7th (D♭)

A

B♭/A♯

B

C

C♯/D♭

D

E♭/D♯

E

F

F♯/G♭

G

A♭/G♯

Other Chords

E♭sus4
E♭ Suspended 4th
(1st position)

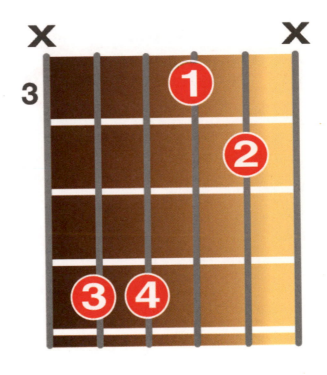

Chord Spelling
1st (E♭), 4th (A♭), 5th (B♭)

E♭sus4
E♭ Suspended 4th
(2nd position)

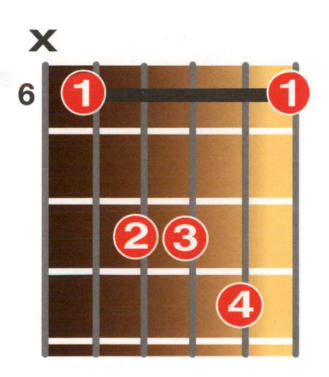

Chord Spelling
1st (E♭), 4th (A♭), 5th (B♭)

A
B♭/A♯
B
C
C♯/D♭
D
E♭/D♯
E
F
F♯/G♭
G
A♭/G♯
Other Chords

E♭7sus4

E♭ Dominant 7th sus4

(1st position)

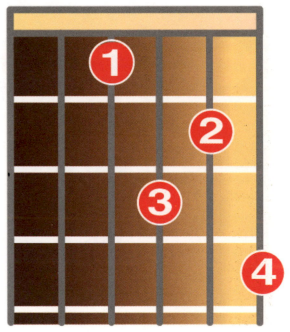

Chord Spelling

1st (E♭), 4th (A♭), 5th (B♭), ♭7th (D♭)

E♭7sus4
E♭ Dominant 7th sus4
(2nd position)

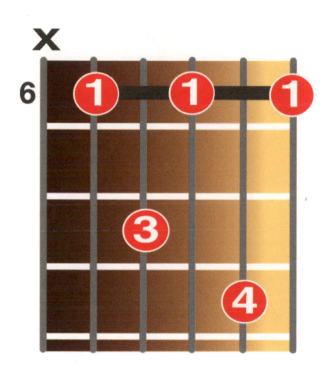

A
B♭/A#
B
C
C#/D♭
D
E♭/D#
E
F
F#/G♭
G
A♭/G#
Other Chords

Chord Spelling
1st (E♭), 4th (A♭), 5th (B♭), ♭7th (D♭)

E♭6
E♭ Major 6th
(1st position)

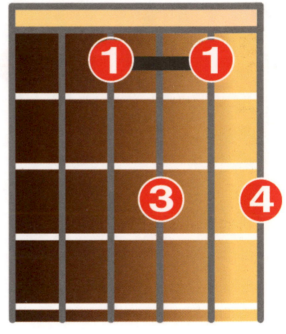

Chord Spelling

1st (E♭), 3rd (G), 5th (B♭), 6th (C)

E♭6

E♭ Major 6th

(2nd position)

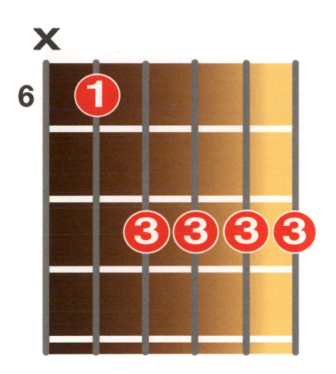

Chord Spelling

1st (E♭), 3rd (G), 5th (B♭), 6th (C)

E♭m6
E♭ Minor 6th

(1st position)

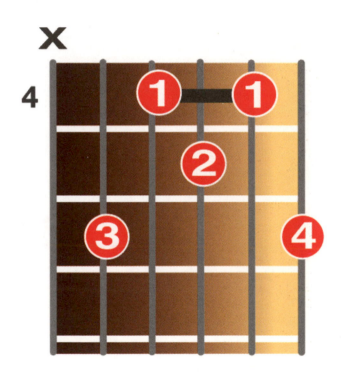

Chord Spelling

1st (E♭), ♭3rd (G♭), 5th (B♭), 6th (C)

E♭m6

E♭ Minor 6th

(2nd position)

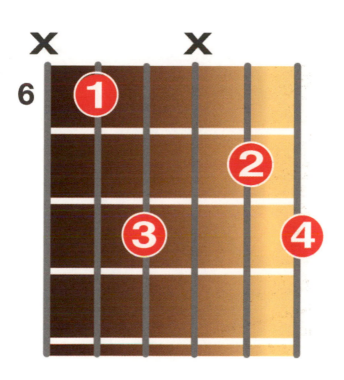

A

B♭/A♯

B

C

C♯/D♭

D

E♭/D♯

E

F

F♯/G♭

G

A♭/G♯

Other Chords

Chord Spelling

1st (E♭), ♭3rd (G♭), 5th (B♭), 6th (C)

E♭7

E♭ Dominant 7th

(1st position)

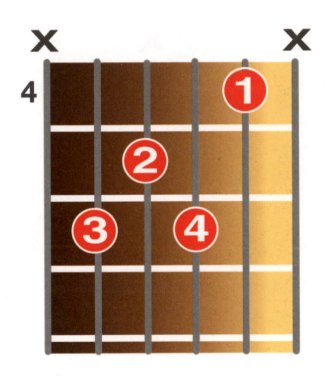

Chord Spelling

1st (E♭), 3rd (G), 5th (B♭), ♭7th (D♭)

A
B♭/A#
B
C
C#/D♭
D
E♭/D#
E
F
F#/G♭
G
A♭/G#
Other Chords

E♭7

E♭ Dominant 7th

(2nd position)

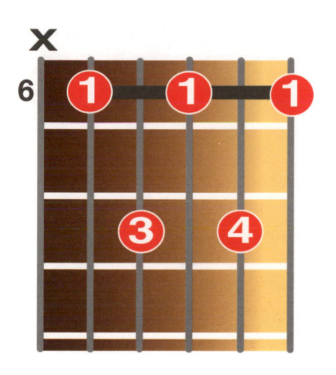

Chord Spelling

1st (E♭), 3rd (G), 5th (B♭), ♭7th (D♭)

A

B♭/A♯

B

C

C♯/D♭

D

E♭/D♯

E

F

F♯/G♭

G

A♭/G♯

Other Chords

E♭9

E♭ Dominant 9th

(1st position)

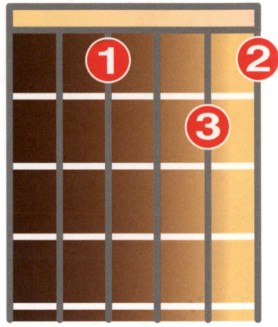

Chord Spelling

1st (E♭), 3rd (G), 5th (B♭), ♭7th (D♭), 9th (F)

A
B♭/A♯
B
C
C♯/D♭
D
E♭/D♯
E
F
F♯/G♭
G
A♭/G♯
Other Chords

E♭9

E♭ Dominant 9th

(2nd position)

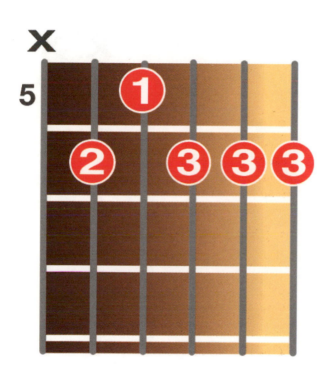

5

Chord Spelling

1st (E♭), 3rd (G), 5th (B♭), ♭7th (D♭), 9th (F)

A
B♭/A♯
B
C
C♯/D♭
D
E♭/D♯
E
F
F♯/G♭
G
A♭/G♯
Other Chords

E♭5

E♭ 5th 'power chord'

(1st position)

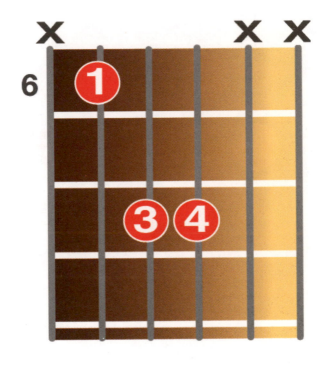

Chord Spelling

1st (E♭), 5th (B♭)

E♭⁶₉

E♭ Major 6th add 9th

(1st position)

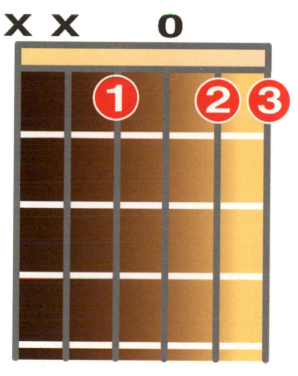

Chord Spelling

1st (E♭), 3rd (G), 5th (B♭), 6th (C), 9th (F)

A

B♭/A♯

B

C

C♯/D♭

D

E♭/D♯

E

F

F♯/G♭

G

A♭/G♯

Other Chords

E♭11
E♭ Dominant 11th
(1st position)

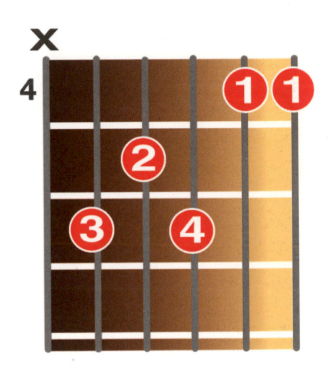

Chord Spelling

1st (E♭), 3rd (G), 5th (B♭), ♭7th (D♭), 9th (F), 11th (A♭)

E♭13
E♭ Dominant 13th
(1st position)

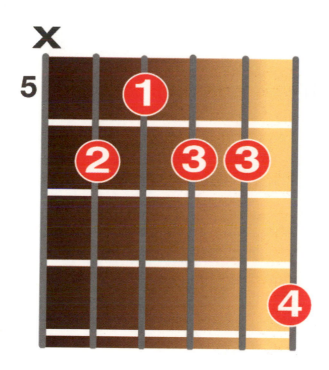

Chord Spelling
st (E♭), 3rd (G), 5th (B♭), ♭7th (D♭), 9th (F), 13th (C)

A
B♭/A#
B
C
C#/D♭
D
E♭/D#
E
F
F#/G♭
G
A♭/G#
Other Chords

E♭add9
E♭ Major add 9th
(1st position)

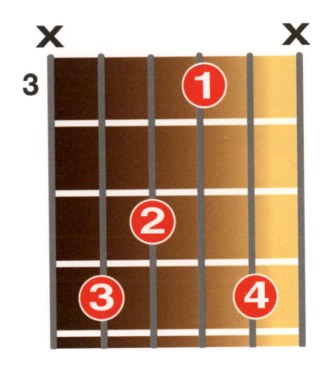

Chord Spelling
1st (E♭), 3rd (G), 5th (B♭), 9th (F)

A
B♭/A♯
B
C
C♯/D♭
D
E♭/D♯
E
F
F♯/G♭
G
A♭/G♯
Other Chords

E♭m9
E♭ Minor 9th

(1st position)

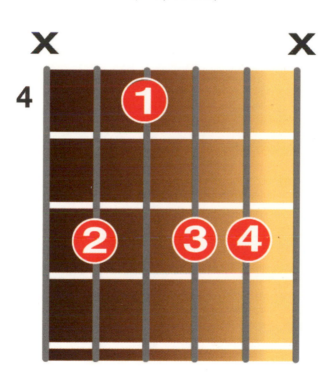

Chord Spelling

1st (E♭), ♭3rd (G♭), 5th (B♭), ♭7th (D♭), 9th (F)

A
B♭/A#
B
C
C#/D♭
D
E♭/D#
E
F
F#/G♭
G
A♭/G#
Other Chords

E♭maj9
E♭ Major 9th
(1st position)

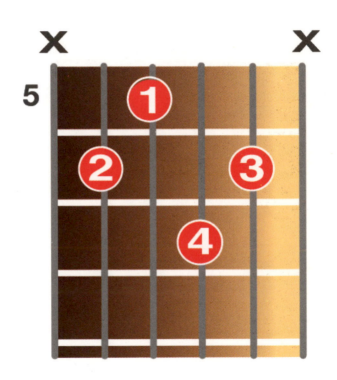

Chord Spelling
1st (E♭), 3rd (G), 5th (B♭), 7th (D), 9th (F)

A
B♭/A#
B
C
C#/D♭
D
E♭/D#
E
F
F#/G♭
G
A♭/G#
Other Chords

E♭+
E♭ Augmented
(1st position)

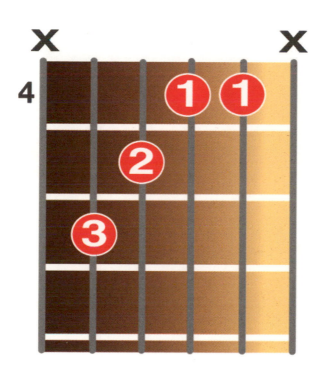

Chord Spelling
1st (E♭), 3rd (G), #5th (B)

A
B♭/A#
B
C
C#/D♭
D
E♭/D#
E
F
F#/G♭
G
A♭/G#
Other Chords

E♭⁰⁷

E♭ Diminished 7th

(1st position)

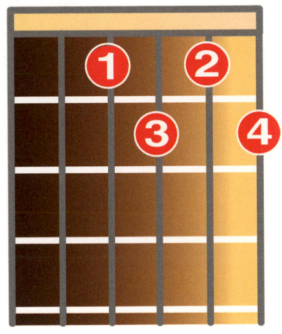

Chord Spelling

1st (E♭), ♭3rd (G♭), ♭5th (B♭♭), ♭♭7th (D♭♭)

E♭⁰

E♭ Diminished triad

(1st position)

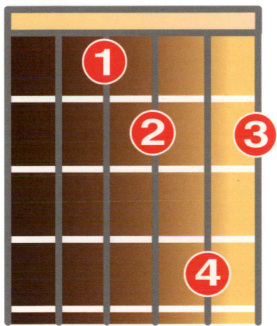

Chord Spelling

1st (E♭), ♭3rd (G♭), ♭5th (B♭♭)

A
B♭/A♯
B
C
C♯/D♭
D
E♭/D♯
E
F
F♯/G♭
G
A♭/G♯
Other Chords

A
B♭/A♯
B
C
C♯/D♭
D
E♭/D♯
E
F
F♯/G♭
G
A♭/G♯
Other Chords

E
E Major

(1st position)

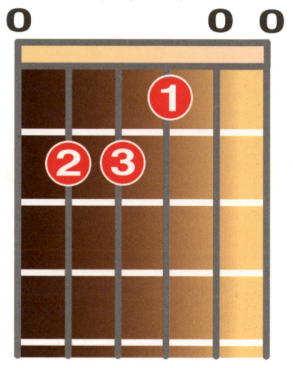

Chord Spelling

1st (E), 3rd (G♯), 5th (B)

E
E Major
(2nd position)

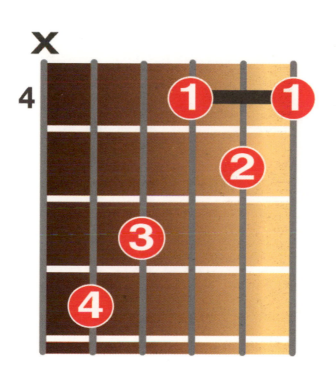

A

B♭/A♯

B

C

C♯/D♭

D

E♭/D♯

E

F

F♯/G♭

G

A♭/G♯

Other Chords

Chord Spelling

1st (E), 3rd (G♯), 5th (B)

A
B♭/A♯
B
C
C♯/D♭
D
E♭/D♯
E
F
F♯/G♭
G
A♭/G♯
Other Chords

Em
E Minor

(1st position)

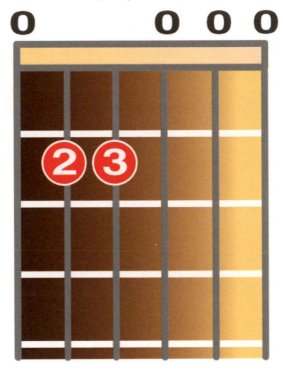

Chord Spelling

1st (E), ♭3rd (G), 5th (B)

Em
E Minor

(2nd position)

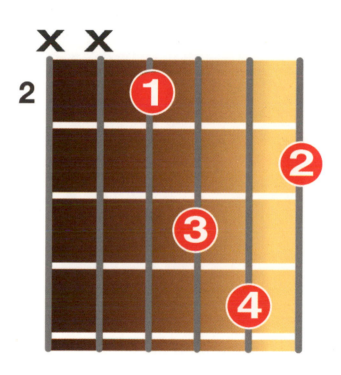

A
B♭/A♯
B
C
C♯/D♭
D
E♭/D♯
E
F
F♯/G♭
G
A♭/G♯
Other Chords

Chord Spelling
1st (E), ♭3rd (G), 5th (B)

Emaj7
E Major 7th
(1st position)

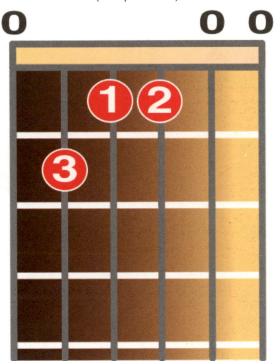

Chord Spelling
1st (E), 3rd (G#), 5th (B), 7th (D#)

A
Bb/A#
B
C
C#/Db
D
Eb/D#
E
F
F#/Gb
G
Ab/G#
Other Chords

Emaj7
E Major 7th
(2nd position)

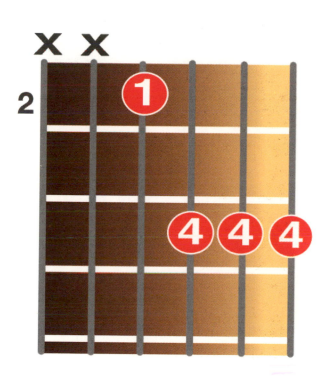

A
Bb/A#
B
C
C#/Db
D
Eb/D#
E
F
F#/Gb
G
Ab/G#
Other Chords

Chord Spelling
1st (E), 3rd (G#), 5th (B), 7th (D#)

Em7
E Minor 7th

(1st position)

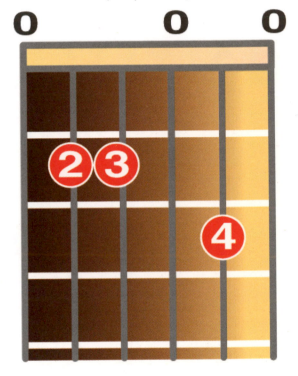

Chord Spelling

1st (E), ♭3rd (G), 5th (B), ♭7th (D)

Em7
E Minor 7th

(2nd position)

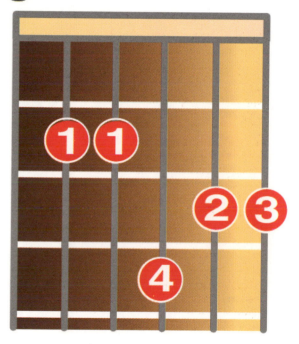

Chord Spelling

1st (E), ♭3rd (G), 5th (B), ♭7th (D)

A

B♭/A♯

B

C

C♯/D♭

D

E♭/D♯

E

F

F♯/G♭

G

A♭/G♯

Other Chords

Esus4
E Suspended 4th

(1st position)

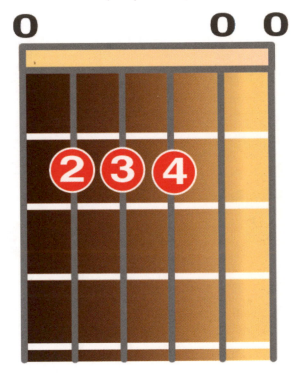

Chord Spelling

1st (E), 4th (A), 5th (B)

Esus4

E Suspended 4th

(2nd position)

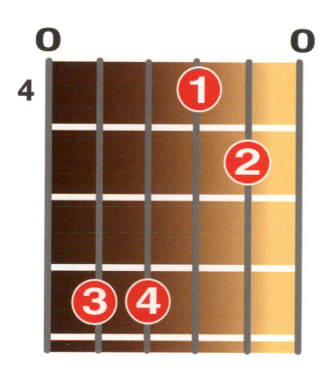

Chord Spelling

1st (E), 4th (A), 5th (B)

A
B♭/A♯
B
C
C♯/D♭
D
E♭/D♯
E
F
F♯/G♭
G
A♭/G♯
Other Chords

E7sus4
E Dominant 7th sus4

(1st position)

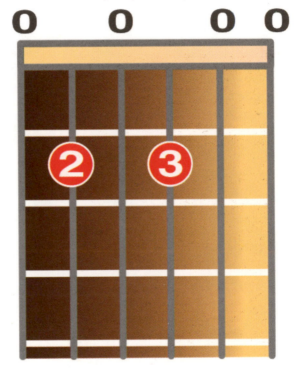

Chord Spelling

1st (E), 4th (A), 5th (B), ♭7th (D)

E7sus4
E Dominant 7th sus4
(2nd position)

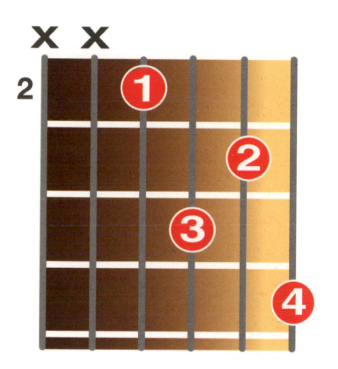

Chord Spelling

1st (E), 4th (A), 5th (B), ♭7th (D)

A
B♭/A♯
B
C
C♯/D♭
D
E♭/D♯
E
F
F♯/G♭
G
A♭/G♯
Other Chords

A
B♭/A♯
B
C
C♯/D♭
D
E♭/D♯
E
F
F♯/G♭
G
A♭/G♯
Other Chords

E6
E Major 6th
(1st position)

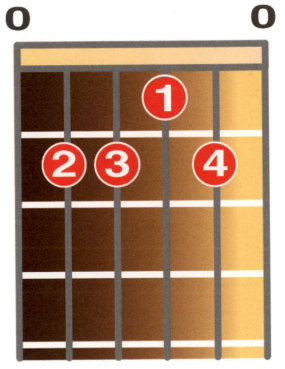

Chord Spelling
1st (E), 3rd (G♯), 5th (B), 6th (C♯)

E6
E Major 6th
(2nd position)

O

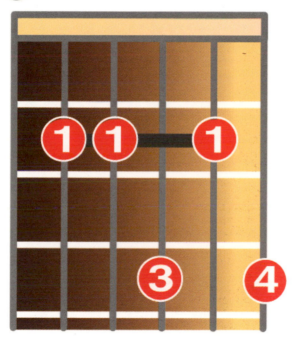

A
Bb/A#
B
C
C#/Db
D
Eb/D#
E
F
F#/Gb
G
Ab/G#
Other
Chords

Chord Spelling

1st (E), 3rd (G#), 5th (B), 6th (C#)

A
B♭/A♯
B
C
C♯/D♭
D
E♭/D♯
E
F
F♯/G♭
G
A♭/G♯
Other Chords

Em6
E Minor 6th

(1st position)

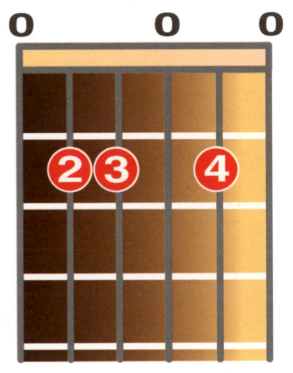

Chord Spelling

1st (E), ♭3rd (G), 5th (B), 6th (C♯)

Em6
E Minor 6th

(2nd position)

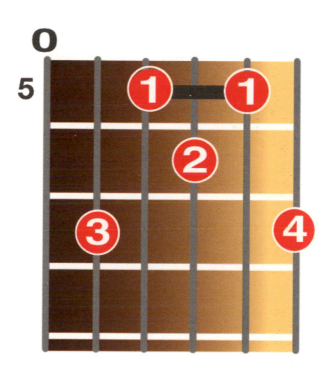

A
B♭/A♯
B
C
C♯/D♭
D
E♭/D♯
E
F
F♯/G♭
G
A♭/G♯
Other Chords

Chord Spelling

1st (E), ♭3rd (G), 5th (B), 6th (C♯)

E7
E Dominant 7th

(1st position)

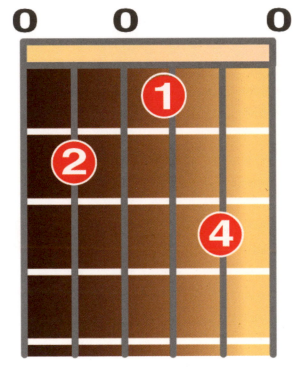

Chord Spelling

1st (E), 3rd (G#), 5th (B), ♭7th (D)

E7
E Dominant 7th

(2nd position)

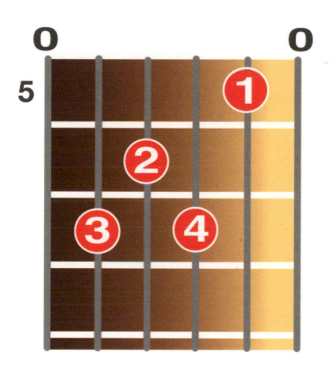

A
B♭/A♯
B
C
C♯/D♭
D
E♭/D♯
E
F
F♯/G♭
G
A♭/G♯
Other Chords

Chord Spelling

1st (E), 3rd (G♯), 5th (B), ♭7th (D)

E9

E Dominant 9th

(1st position)

Chord Spelling

1st (E), 3rd (G#), 5th (B), ♭7th (D), 9th (F#)

E9
E Dominant 9th
(2nd position)

A
B♭/A♯
B
C
C♯/D♭
D
E♭/D♯
E
F
F♯/G♭
G
A♭/G♯
Other Chords

O

6

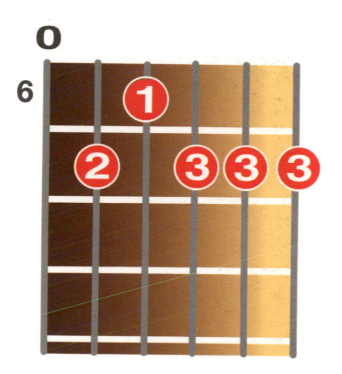

Chord Spelling
1st (E), 3rd (G♯), 5th (B), ♭7th (D), 9th (F♯)

E5

E 5th 'power chord'

(1st position)

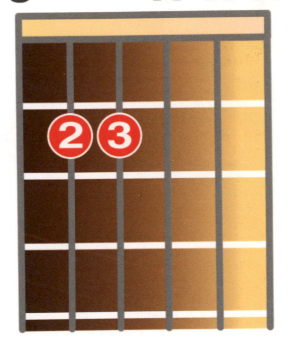

Chord Spelling

1st (E), 5th (B)

A

B♭/A♯

B

C

C♯/D♭

D

E♭/D♯

E

F

F♯/G♭

G

A♭/G♯

Other Chords

E$^6_9$
E Major 6th add 9th

(1st position)

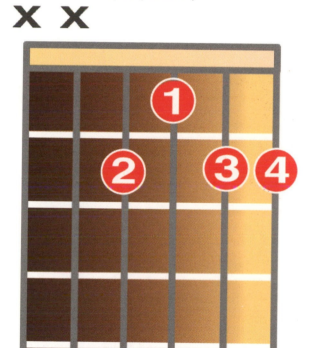

Chord Spelling

1st (E), 3rd (G#), 5th (B), 6th (C#), 9th (F#)

A

B♭/A#

B

C

C#/D♭

D

E♭/D#

E

F

F#/G♭

G

A♭/G#

Other Chords

E11
E Dominant 11th
(1st position)

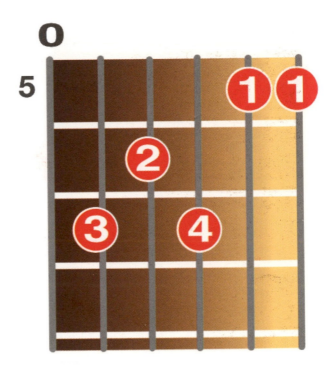

Chord Spelling
1st (E), 3rd (G#), 5th (B), ♭7th (D), 9th (F#), 11th (A)

A
B♭/A#
B
C
C#/D♭
D
E♭/D#
E
F
F#/G♭
G
A♭/G#
Other Chords

E13
E Dominant 13th
(1st position)

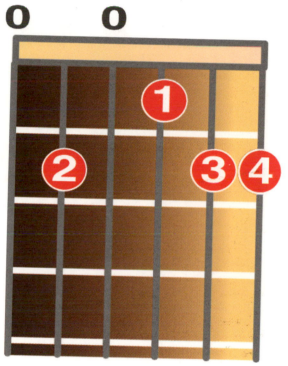

A

B♭/A♯

B

C

C♯/D♭

D

E♭/D♯

E

F

F♯/G♭

G

A♭/G♯

Other Chords

Chord Spelling

t (E), ♭3rd (G), 5th (B), ♭7th (D), 9th (F♯), 13th (C♯)

Eadd9
E Major add 9th

(1st position)

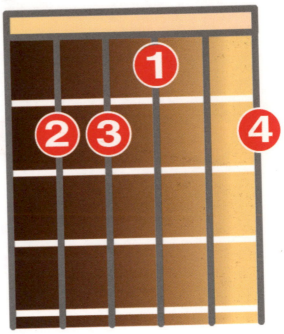

Chord Spelling

1st (E), 3rd (G#), 5th (B), 9th (F#)

Em9
E Minor 9th
(1st position)

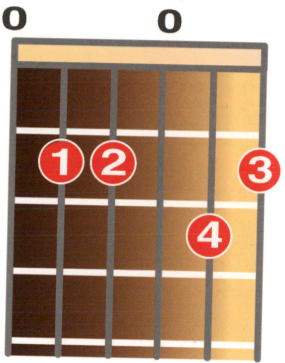

A
B♭/A♯
B
C
C♯/D♭
D
E♭/D♯
E
F
F♯/G♭
G
A♭/G♯
Other Chords

Chord Spelling

1st (E), ♭3rd (G), 5th (B), ♭7th (D), 9th (F♯)

Emaj9
E Major 9th

(1st position)

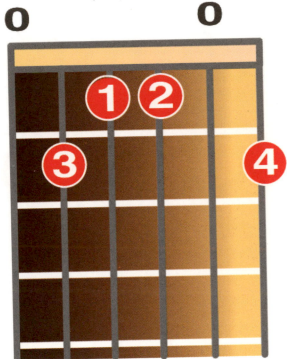

Chord Spelling

1st (E), 3rd (G#), 5th (B), 7th (D#), 9th (F#)

E+
E Augmented
(1st position)

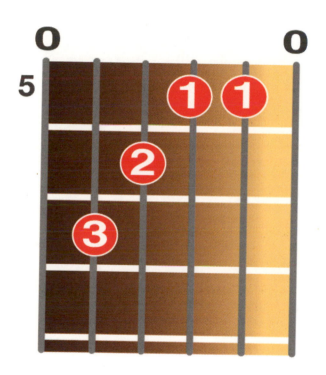

Chord Spelling
1st (E), 3rd (G#), #5th (B#)

A
Bb/A#
B
C
C#/Db
D
Eb/D#
E
F
F#/Gb
G
Ab/G#
Other Chords

A
B♭/A♯
B
C
C♯/D♭
D
E♭/D♯
E
F
F♯/G♭
G
A♭/G♯
Other
Chords

E⁰⁷

E Diminished 7th

(1st position)

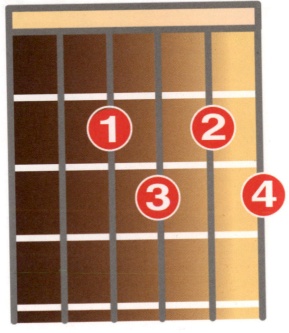

Chord Spelling

1st (E), ♭3rd (G), ♭5th (B♭), ♭♭7th (D♭)

E⁰

E Diminished triad

(1st position)

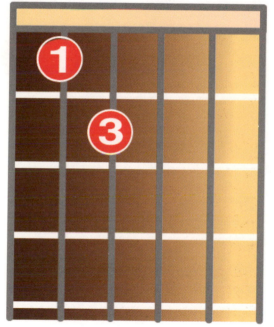

Chord Spelling

1st (E), ♭3rd (G), ♭5th (B♭)

A
B♭/A♯
B
C
C♯/D♭
D
E♭/D♯
E
F
F♯/G♭
G
A♭/G♯
Other Chords

F

F Major

(1st position)

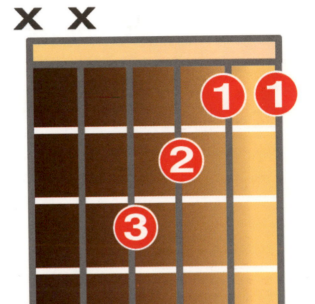

Chord Spelling

1st (F), 3rd (A), 5th (C)

A
Bb/A#
B
C
C#/Db
D
Eb/D#
E
F
F#/Gb
G
Ab/G#
Other Chords

F

F Major

(2nd position)

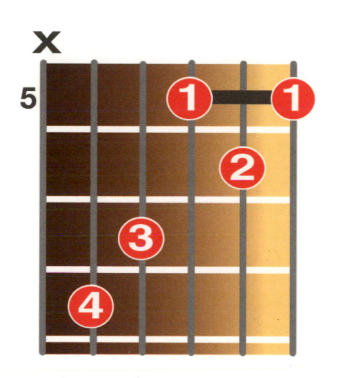

A
Bb/A#
B
C
C#/Db
D
Eb/D#
E
F
F#/Gb
G
Ab/G#
Other Chords

Chord Spelling

1st (F), 3rd (A), 5th (C)

Fm
F Minor
(1st position)

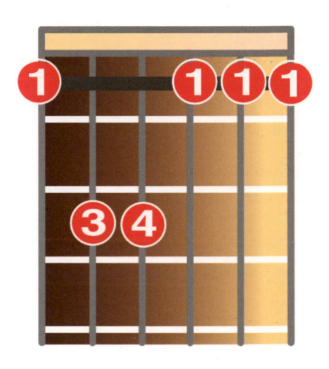

Chord Spelling
1st (F), ♭3rd (A♭), 5th (C)

A
B♭/A♯
B
C
C♯/D♭
D
E♭/D♯
E
F
F♯/G♭
G
A♭/G♯
Other Chords

Fm
F Minor
(2nd position)

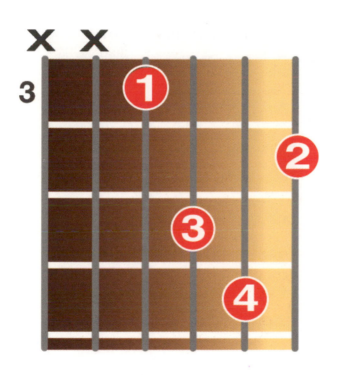

A
B♭/A♯
B
C
C♯/D♭
D
E♭/D♯
E
F
F♯/G♭
G
A♭/G♯
Other Chords

Chord Spelling
1st (F), ♭3rd (A♭), 5th (C)

Fmaj7
F Major 7th

(1st position)

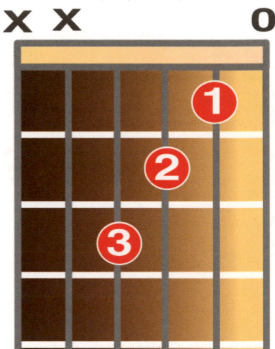

Chord Spelling

1st (F), 3rd (A), 5th (C), 7th (E)

A
Bb/A#
B
C
C#/Db
D
Eb/D#
E
F
F#/Gb
G
Ab/G#
Other Chords

Fmaj7
F Major 7th
(2nd position)

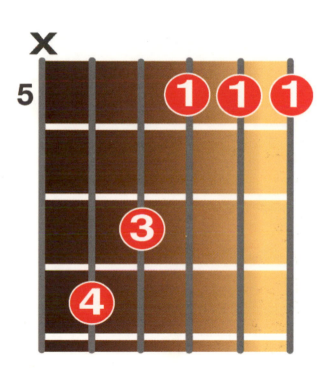

Chord Spelling
1st (F), 3rd (A), 5th (C), 7th (E)

A

Bb/A#

B

C

C#/Db

D

Eb/D#

E

F

F#/Gb

G

Ab/G#

Other
Chords

Fm7
F Minor 7th
(1st position)

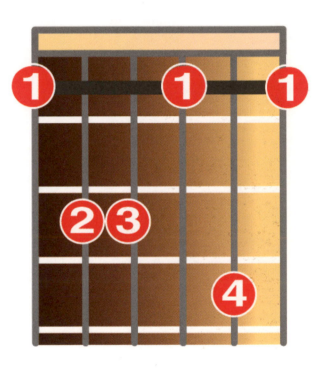

Chord Spelling
1st (F), ♭3rd (A♭), 5th (C), ♭7th (E♭)

A
B♭/A♯
B
C
C♯/D♭
D
E♭/D♯
E
F
F♯/G♭
G
A♭/G♯
Other Chords

Fm7
F Minor 7th

(2nd position)

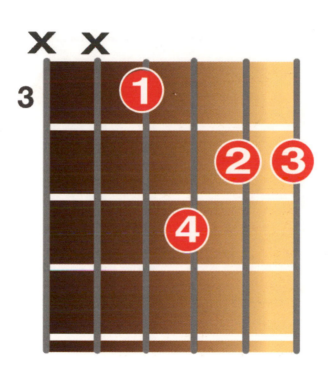

Chord Spelling

1st (F), ♭3rd (A♭), 5th (C), ♭7th (E♭)

A

B♭/A♯

B

C

C♯/D♭

D

E♭/D♯

E

F

F♯/G♭

G

A♭/G♯

Other Chords

Fsus4
F Suspended 4th

(1st position)

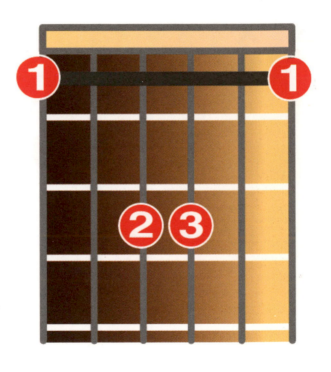

Chord Spelling

1st (F), 4th (B♭), 5th (C)

A
B♭/A♯
B
C
C♯/D♭
D
E♭/D♯
E
F
F♯/G♭
G
A♭/G♯
Other Chords

Fsus4

F Suspended 4th

(2nd position)

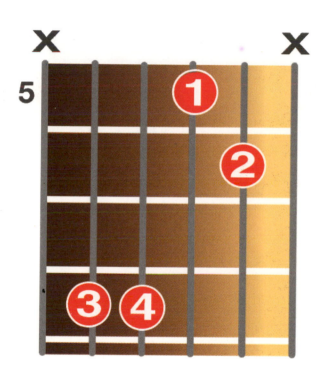

Chord Spelling

1st (F), 4th (B♭), 5th (C)

A

B♭/A♯

B

C

C♯/D♭

D

E♭/D♯

E

F

F♯/G♭

G

A♭/G♯

Other Chords

F7sus4

F Dominant 7th sus4

(1st position)

A

B♭/A♯

B

C

C♯/D♭

D

E♭/D♯

E

F

F♯/G♭

G

A♭/G♯

Other Chords

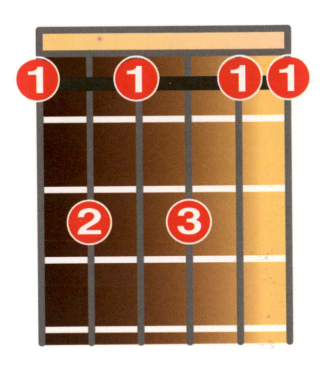

Chord Spelling

1st (F), 4th (B♭), 5th (C), ♭7th (E♭)

F7sus4
F Dominant 7th sus4
(2nd position)

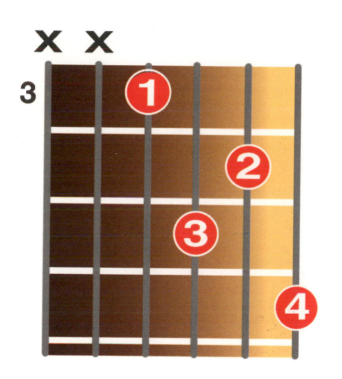

A
B♭/A♯
B
C
C♯/D♭
D
E♭/D♯
E
F
F♯/G♭
G
A♭/G♯
Other Chords

Chord Spelling
1st (F), 4th (B♭), 5th (C), ♭7th (E♭)

F6
F Major 6th
(1st position)

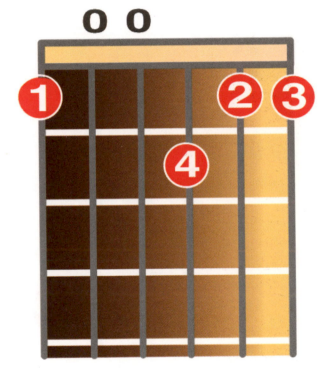

Chord Spelling
1st (F), 3rd (A), 5th (C), 6th (D)

A
B♭/A♯
B
C
C♯/D♭
D
E♭/D♯
E
F
F♯/G♭
G
A♭/G♯
Other Chords

F6
F Major 6th
(2nd position)

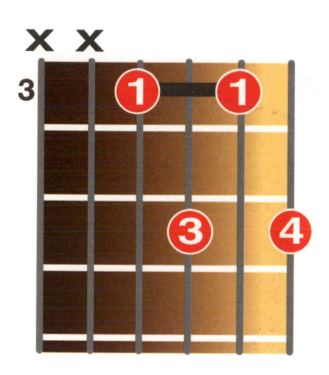

A
B♭/A♯
B
C
C♯/D♭
D
E♭/D♯
E
F
F♯/G♭
G
A♭/G♯
Other Chords

Chord Spelling

1st (F), 3rd (A), 5th (C), 6th (D)

Fm6
F Minor 6th

(1st position)

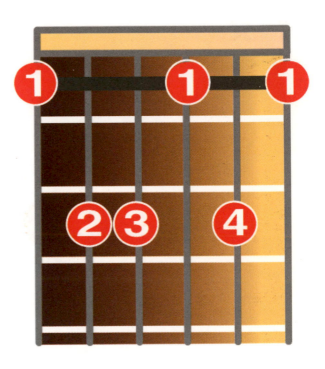

Chord Spelling
1st (F), ♭3rd (A♭), 5th (C), 6th (D)

A
B♭/A#
B
C
C#/D♭
D
E♭/D#
E
F
F#/G♭
G
A♭/G#
Other Chords

Fm6
F Minor 6th
(2nd position)

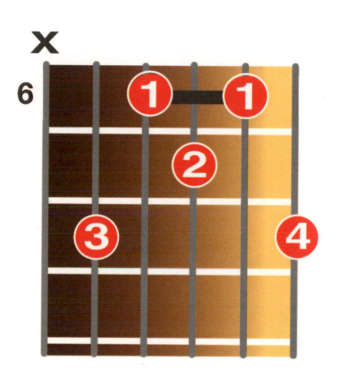

Chord Spelling
1st (F), ♭3rd (A♭), 5th (C), 6th (D)

A
B♭/A♯
B
C
C♯/D♭
D
E♭/D♯
E
F
F♯/G♭
G
A♭/G♯
Other Chords

F7
F Dominant 7th
(1st position)

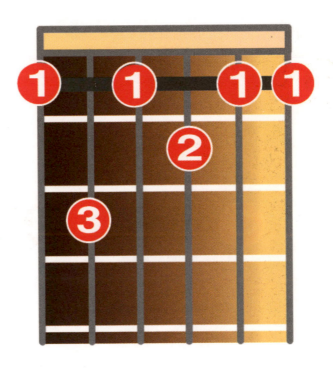

Chord Spelling
1st (F), 3rd (A), 5th (C), ♭7th (E♭)

F7

F Dominant 7th

(2nd position)

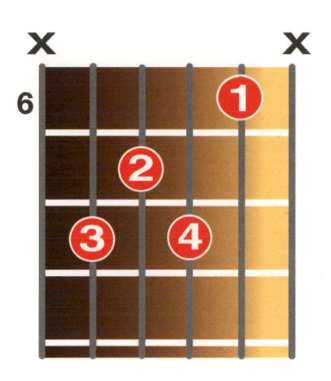

6

X   X

Chord Spelling

1st (F), 3rd (A), 5th (C), ♭7th (E♭)

A

B♭/A♯

B

C

C♯/D♭

D

E♭/D♯

E

F

F♯/G♭

G

A♭/G♯

Other Chords

F9
F Dominant 9th
(1st position)

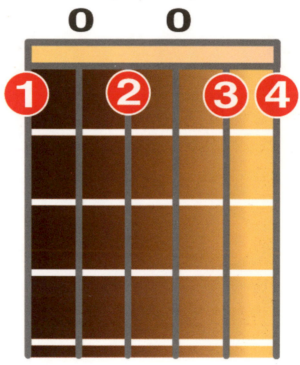

Chord Spelling
1st (F), 3rd (A), 5th (C), ♭7th (E♭), 9th (G)

A
B♭/A♯
B
C
C♯/D♭
D
E♭/D♯
E
F
F♯/G♭
G
A♭/G♯
Other Chords

F9

F Dominant 9th

(2nd position)

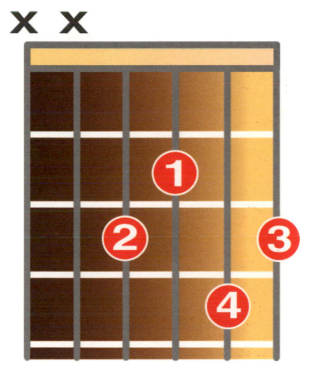

Chord Spelling

1st (F), 3rd (A), 5th (C), ♭7th (E♭), 9th (G)

A
B♭/A♯
B
C
C♯/D♭
D
E♭/D♯
E
F
F♯/G♭
G
A♭/G♯
Other Chords

F5

F 5th 'power chord'

(1st position)

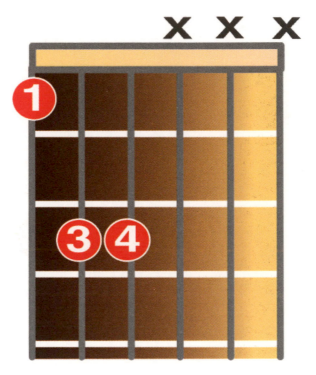

Chord Spelling

1st (F), 5th (C)

A
B♭/A♯
B
C
C♯/D♭
D
E♭/D♯
E
F
F♯/G♭
G
A♭/G♯
Other Chords

F⁶₉

F Major 6th add 9th

(1st position)

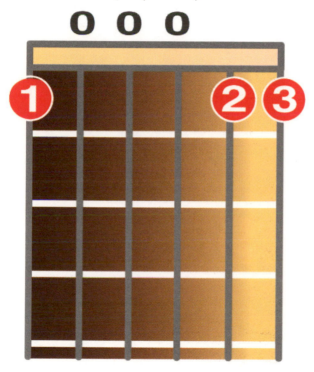

A

B♭/A♯

B

C

C♯/D♭

D

E♭/D♯

E

F

F♯/G♭

G

A♭/G♯

Other Chords

Chord Spelling

1st (F), 3rd (A), 5th (C), 6th (D), 9th (D)

F11
F Dominant 11th
(1st position)

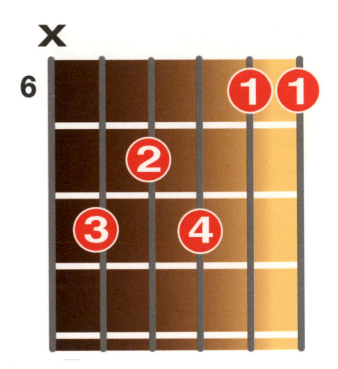

Chord Spelling
1st (F), 3rd (A), 5th (C), ♭7th (E♭), 9th (G), 11th (B♭)

F13

F Dominant 13th

(1st position)

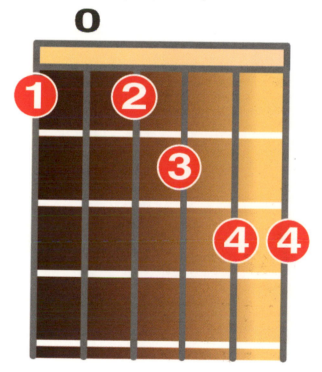

Chord Spelling

1st (F), 3rd (A), 5th (C), ♭7th (E♭), 9th (G), 13th (D)

A

B♭/A♯

B

C

C♯/D♭

D

E♭/D♯

E

F

F♯/G♭

G

A♭/G♯

Other Chords

A
B♭/A♯
B
C
C♯/D♭
D
E♭/D♯
E
F
F♯/G♭
G
A♭/G♯
Other Chords

Fadd9
F Major add 9th
(1st position)

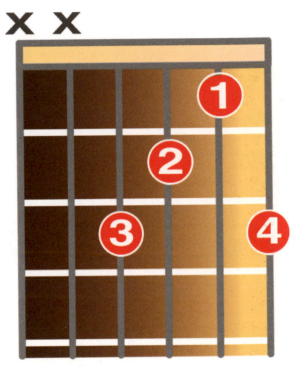

Chord Spelling

1st (F), 3rd (A), 5th (C), 9th (G)

Fm9
F Minor 9th

(1st position)

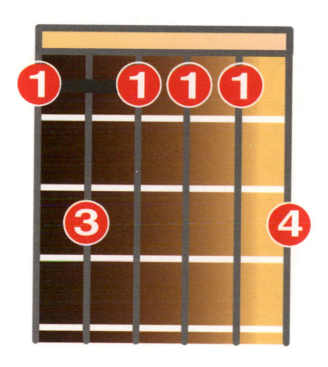

A
Bb/A#
B
C
C#/Db
D
Eb/D#
E
F
F#/Gb
G
Ab/G#
Other
Chords

Chord Spelling

1st (F), b3rd (Ab), 5th (C), b7th (Eb), 9th (G)

Fmaj9
F Major 9th

(1st position)

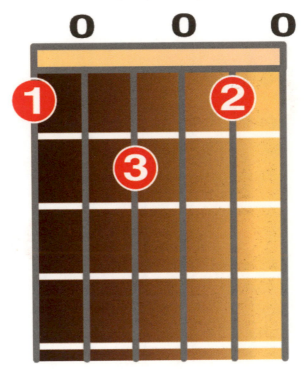

Chord Spelling

1st (F), 3rd (A), 5th (C), 7th (E), 9th (G)

A

B♭/A♯

B

C

C♯/D♭

D

E♭/D♯

E

F

F♯/G♭

G

A♭/G♯

Other Chords

F+

F Augmented

(1st position)

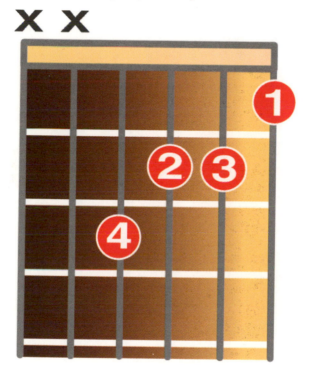

Chord Spelling

1st (F), 3rd (A), #5th (C#)

A

B♭/A♯

B

C

C♯/D♭

D

E♭/D♯

E

F

F♯/G♭

G

A♭/G♯

Other Chords

F⁰⁷
F Diminished 7th

(1st position)

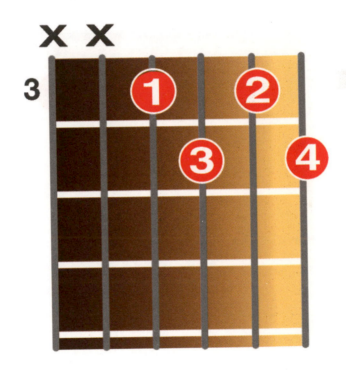

Chord Spelling

1st (F), ♭3rd (A♭), ♭5th (C♭), ♭♭7th (E♭♭)

F⁰

F Diminished triad

(1st position)

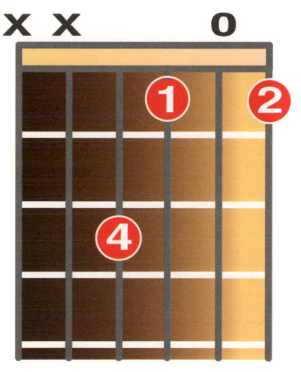

A
B♭/A♯
B
C
C♯/D♭
D
E♭/D♯
E
F
F♯/G♭
G
A♭/G♯
Other Chords

Chord Spelling

1st (F), ♭3rd (A♭), ♭5th (C♭)

F♯
F♯ Major
(1st position)

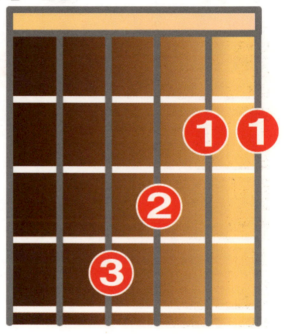

Chord Spelling
1st (F#), 3rd (A#), 5th (C#)

F#

F# Major

(2nd position)

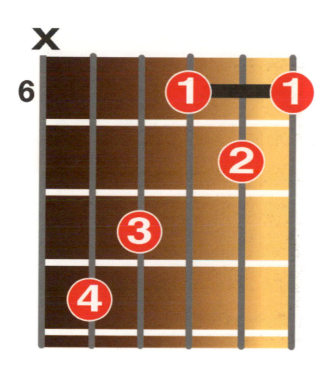

X

6

1 1

2

3

4

A
Bb/A#
B
C
C#/Db
D
Eb/D#
E
F
F#/Gb
G
Ab/G#
Other Chords

Chord Spelling

1st (F#), 3rd (A#), 5th (C#)

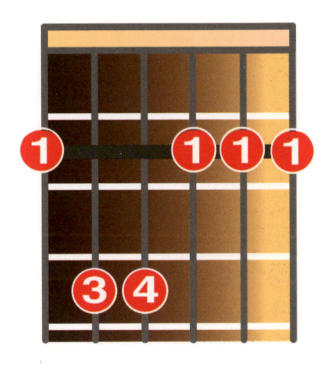

F#m
F# Minor

(1st position)

Chord Spelling

1st (F#), ♭3rd (A), 5th (C#)

A

B♭/A#

B

C

C#/D♭

D

E♭/D#

E

F

F#/G♭

G

A♭/G#

Other Chords

F#m

F# Minor

(2nd position)

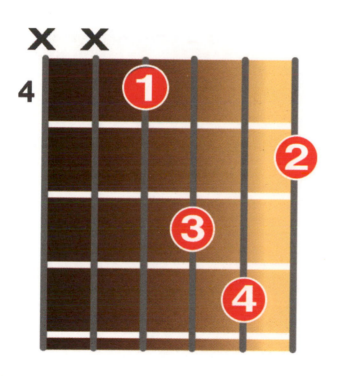

Chord Spelling

1st (F#), ♭3rd (A), 5th (C#)

A

B♭/A#

B

C

C#/D♭

D

E♭/D#

E

F

F#/G♭

G

A♭/G#

Other Chords

F#maj7
F# Major 7th

(1st position)

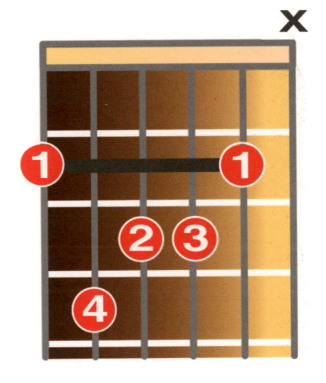

Chord Spelling

1st (F#), 3rd (A#), 5th (C#), 7th (E#)

F#maj7
F# Major 7th

(2nd position)

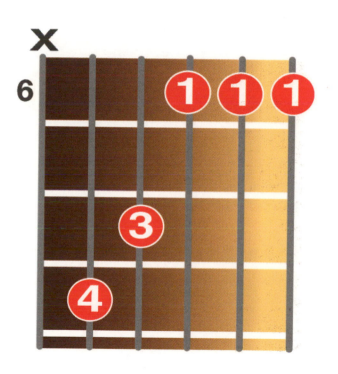

Chord Spelling

1st (F#), 3rd (A#), 5th (C#), 7th (E#)

A
B♭/A#
B
C
C#/D♭
D
E♭/D#
E
F
F#/G♭
G
A♭/G#
Other Chords

F♯m7
F♯ Minor 7th
(1st position)

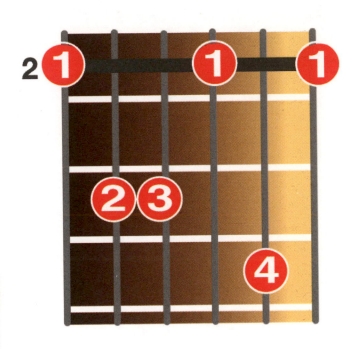

Chord Spelling
1st (F#), ♭3rd (A), 5th (C#), ♭7th (E)

A
B♭/A#
B
C
C#/D♭
D
E♭/D#
E
F
F#/G♭
G
A♭/G#
Other
Chords

F#m7
F# Minor 7th
(2nd position)

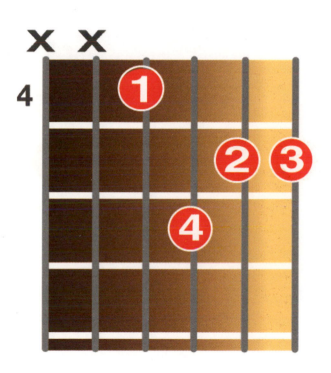

Chord Spelling
1st (F#), b3rd (A), 5th (C#), b7th (E)

A
Bb/A#
B
C
C#/Db
D
Eb/D#
E
F
F#/Gb
G
Ab/G#
Other Chords

F♯sus4
F♯ Suspended 4th

(1st position)

A
B♭/A♯
B
C
C♯/D♭
D
E♭/D♯
E
F
F♯/G♭
G
A♭/G♯
Other Chords

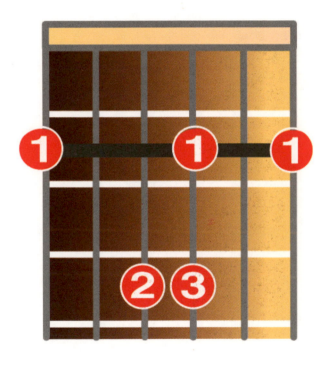

Chord Spelling

1st (F♯), 4th (B), 5th (C♯)

F#sus4

F# Suspended 4th

(2nd position)

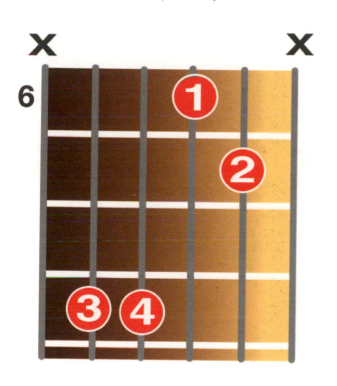

Chord Spelling

1st (F♯), 4th (B), 5th (C♯)

F#7sus4

F# Dominant 7th sus4

(1st position)

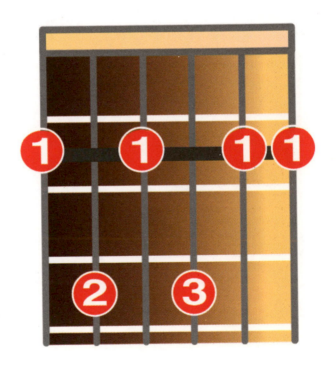

Chord Spelling

1st (F#), 4th (B), 5th (C#), ♭7th (E)

F♯7sus4
F♯ Dominant 7th sus4

(2nd position)

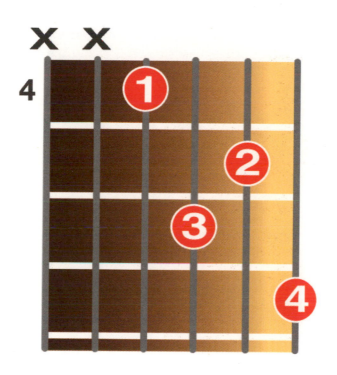

A
B♭/A♯
B
C
C♯/D♭
D
E♭/D♯
E
F
F♯/G♭
G
A♭/G♯
Other Chords

Chord Spelling

1st (F♯), 4th (B), 5th (C♯), ♭7th (E)

F#6
F# Major 6th
(1st position)

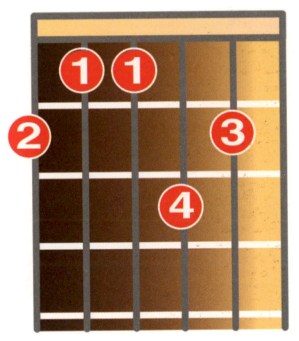

Chord Spelling
1st (F#), 3rd (A#), 5th (C#), 6th (D#)

F#6
F# Major 6th
(2nd position)

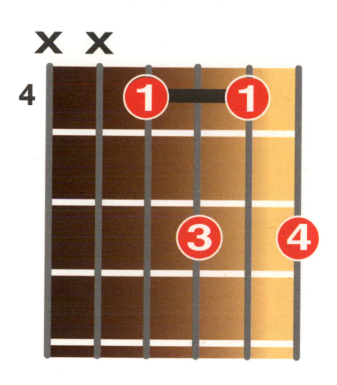

A
B♭/A#
B
C
C#/D♭
D
E♭/D#
E
F
F#/G♭
G
A♭/G#
Other Chords

Chord Spelling

1st (F#), 3rd (A#), 5th (C#), 6th (D#)

F#m6
F# Minor 6th

(1st position)

A

Bb/A#

B

C

C#/Db

D

Eb/D#

E

F

F#/Gb

G

Ab/G#

Other Chords

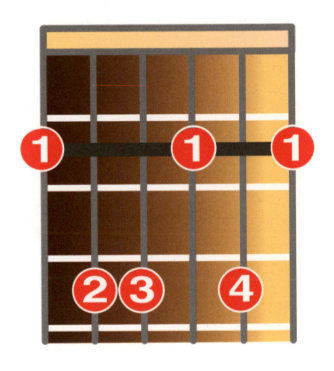

Chord Spelling

1st (F#), b3rd (A), 5th (C#), 6th (D#)

F#m6
F# Minor 6th
(2nd position)

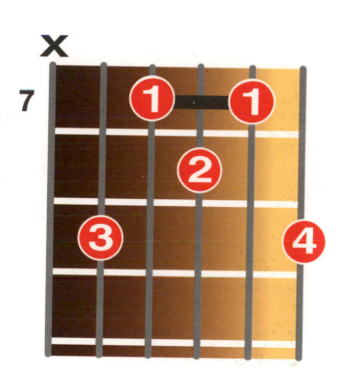

Chord Spelling
1st (F#), ♭3rd (A), 5th (C#), 6th (D#)

A

B♭/A#

B

C

C#/D♭

D

E♭/D#

E

F

F#/G♭

G

A♭/G#

Other
Chords

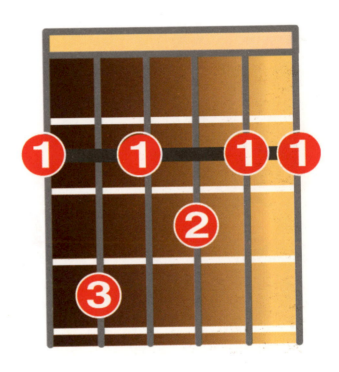

F#7

F# Dominant 7th

(1st position)

Chord Spelling

1st (F#), 3rd (A#), 5th (C#), ♭7th (E)

A
B♭/A#
B
C
C#/D♭
D
E♭/D#
E
F
F#/G♭
G
A♭/G#
Other Chords

F#7

F# Dominant 7th

(2nd position)

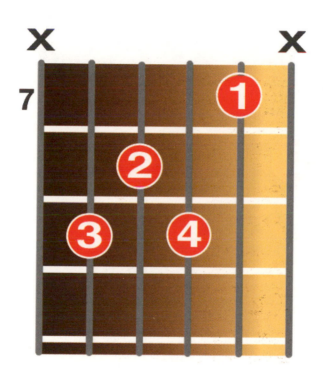

Chord Spelling

1st (F#), 3rd (A#), 5th (C#), ♭7th (E)

A
B♭/A#
B
C
C#/D♭
D
E♭/D#
E
F
F#/G♭
G
A♭/G#
Other Chords

F#9
F# Dominant 9th
(1st position)

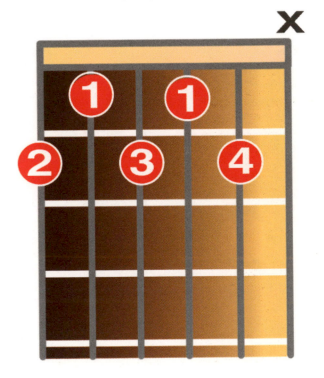

Chord Spelling

1st (F#), 3rd (A#), 5th (C#), ♭7th (E), 9th (G#)

A
B♭/A#
B
C
C#/D♭
D
E♭/D#
E
F
F#/G♭
G
A♭/G#
Other Chords

F#9
F# Dominant 9th
(2nd position)

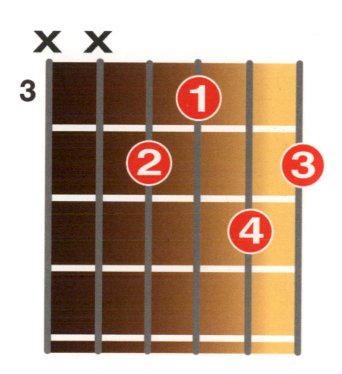

A
B♭/A♯
B
C
C♯/D♭
D
E♭/D♯
E
F
F♯/G♭
G
A♭/G♯
Other Chords

Chord Spelling
1st (F♯), 3rd (A♯), 5th (C♯), ♭7th (E), 9th (G♯)

F#5

F# 5th 'power chord'

(1st position)

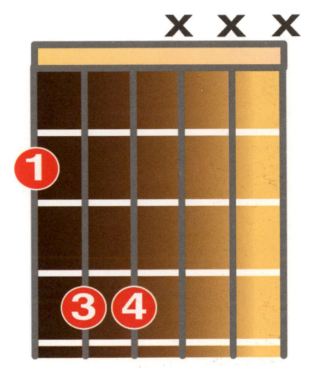

Chord Spelling

1st (F#), 5th (C#)

A
Bb/A#
B
C
C#/Db
D
Eb/D#
E
F
F#/Gb
G
Ab/G#
Other Chords

F#⁶₉

F♯ Major 6th add 9th

(1st position)

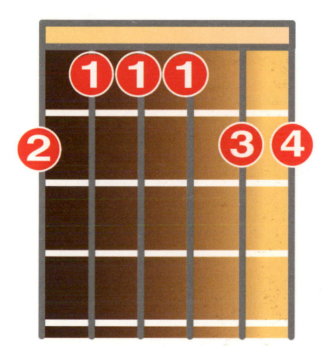

Chord Spelling

1st (F#), 3rd (A#), 5th (C#), 6th (G#), 9th (D#)

A

B♭/A#

B

C

C#/D♭

D

E♭/D#

E

F

F#/G♭

G

A♭/G#

Other Chords

F♯11

F♯ Dominant 11th

(1st position)

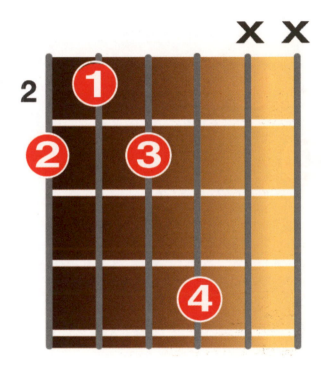

Chord Spelling

1st (F♯), 3rd (A♯), 5th (C♯), ♭7th (E), 9th (G♯), 11th (B)

F#13
F# Dominant 13th
(1st position)

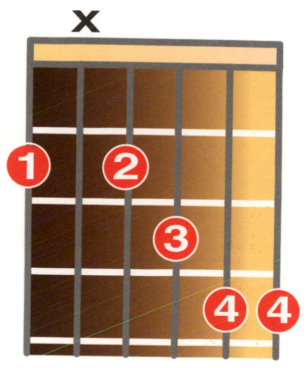

A

B♭/A#

B

C

C#/D♭

D

E♭/D#

E

F

F#/G♭

G

A♭/G#

Other
Chords

Chord Spelling

t (F#), 3rd (A#), 5th (C#), ♭7th (E), 9th (G#), 13th (D#)

F#add9
F# Major add 9th

(1st position)

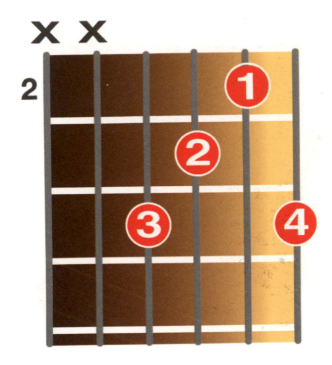

Chord Spelling

1st (F#), 3rd (A#), 5th (C#), 9th (G#)

F#m9
F# Minor 9th

(1st position)

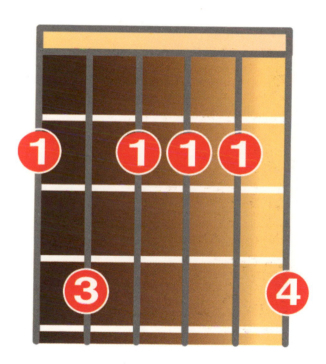

A

B♭/A♯

B

C

C♯/D♭

D

E♭/D♯

E

F

F♯/G♭

G

A♭/G♯

Other Chords

Chord Spelling

1st (F♯), ♭3rd (A), 5th (C♯), ♭7th (E), 9th (G♯)

A

B♭/A♯

B

C

C♯/D♭

D

E♭/D♯

E

F

F♯/G♭

G

A♭/G♯

Other
Chords

F♯maj9
F♯ Major 9th

(1st position)

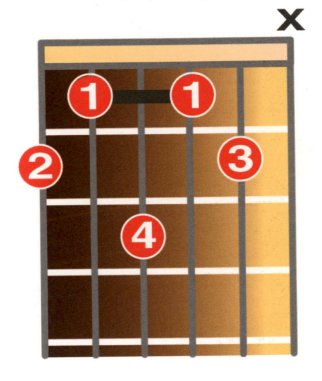

Chord Spelling

1st (F♯), 3rd (A♯), 5th (C♯), 7th (E♯), 9th (G♯)

F#+

F# Augmented

(1st position)

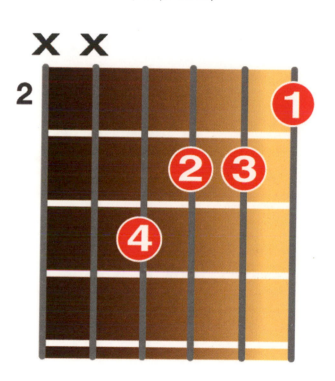

Chord Spelling

1st (F#), 3rd (A#), #5th (Cx)

A

B♭/A#

B

C

C#/D♭

D

E♭/D#

E

F

F#/G♭

G

A♭/G#

Other Chords

F#⁰⁷

F♯ Diminished 7th

(1st position)

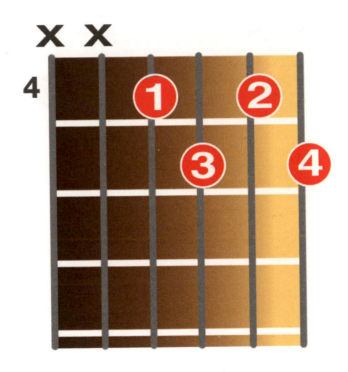

Chord Spelling

1st (F♯), ♭3rd (A), ♭5th (C), ♭♭7th (E♭)

F#°

F# Diminished triad

(1st position)

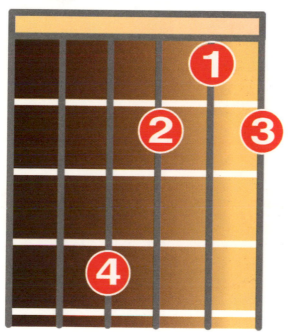

Chord Spelling
1st (F#), ♭3rd (A), ♭5th (C)

A

B♭/A#

B

C

C#/D♭

D

E♭/D#

E

F

F#/G♭

G

A♭/G#

Other
Chords

G

G Major

(1st position)

O O O

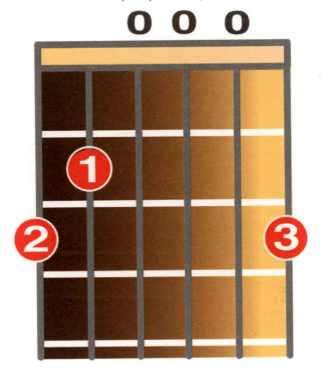

Chord Spelling

1st (G), 3rd (B), 5th (D)

A
B♭/A♯
B
C
C♯/D♭
D
E♭/D♯
E
F
F♯/G♭
G
A♭/G♯
Other Chords

G

G Major

(2nd position)

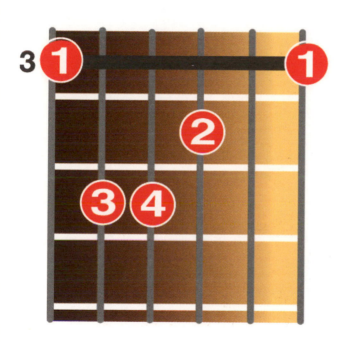

A

B♭/A♯

B

C

C♯/D♭

D

E♭/D♯

E

F

F♯/G♭

G

A♭/G♯

Other Chords

Chord Spelling

1st (G), 3rd (B), 5th (D)

Gm
G Minor

(1st position)

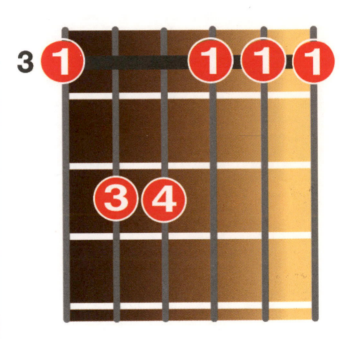

Chord Spelling
1st (G), ♭3rd (B♭), 5th (D)

Gm
G Minor
(2nd position)

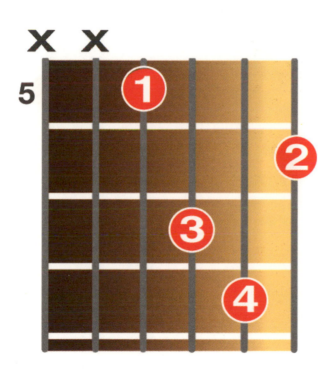

X X

5

Chord Spelling

1st (G), ♭3rd (B♭), 5th (D)

A
B♭/A♯
B
C
C♯/D♭
D
E♭/D♯
E
F
F♯/G♭
G
A♭/G♯
Other Chords

Gmaj7
G Major 7th
(1st position)

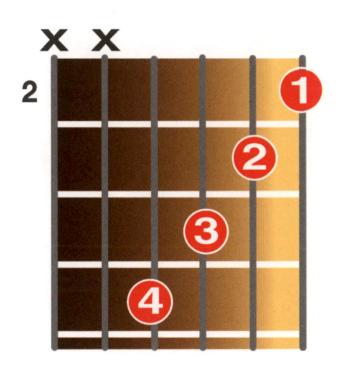

Chord Spelling
1st (G), 3rd (B), 5th (D), 7th (F♯)

A

B♭/A♯

B

C

C♯/D♭

D

E♭/D♯

E

F

F♯/G♭

G

A♭/G♯

Other Chords

Gmaj7
G Major 7th
(2nd position)

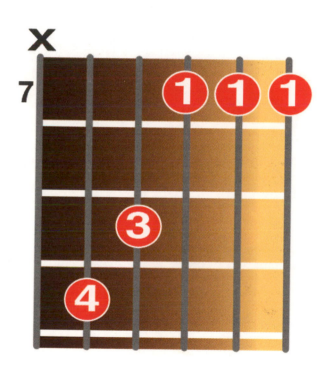

Chord Spelling

1st (G), 3rd (B), 5th (D), 7th (F#)

A
Bb/A#
B
C
C#/Db
D
Eb/D#
E
F
F#/Gb
G
Ab/G#
Other Chords

Gm7
G Minor 7th
(1st position)

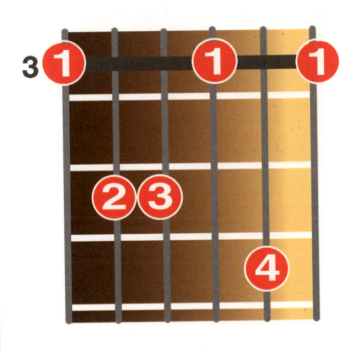

A
B♭/A♯
B
C
C♯/D♭
D
E♭/D♯
E
F
F♯/G♭
G
A♭/G♯
Other Chords

3

Chord Spelling
1st (G), ♭3rd (B♭), 5th (D), ♭7th (F)

Gm7
G Minor 7th
(2nd position)

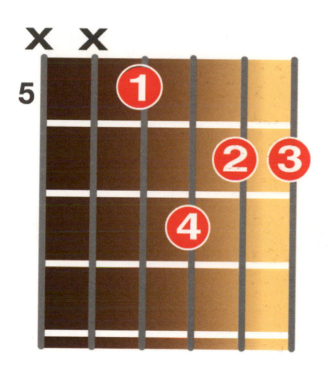

Chord Spelling
1st (G), ♭3rd (B♭), 5th (D), ♭7th (F)

A
B♭/A♯
B
C
C♯/D♭
D
E♭/D♯
E
F
F♯/G♭
G
A♭/G♯
Other Chords

Gsus4
G Suspended 4th

(1st position)

X O O

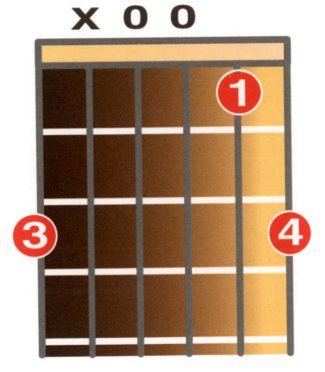

Chord Spelling

1st (G), 4th (C), 5th (D)

A
B♭/A♯
B
C
C♯/D♭
D
E♭/D♯
E
F
F♯/G♭
G
A♭/G♯
Other Chords

Gsus4
G Suspended 4th
(2nd position)

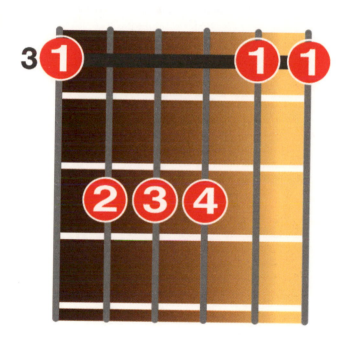

Chord Spelling
1st (G), 4th (C), 5th (D)

A

B♭/A♯

B

C

C♯/D♭

D

E♭/D♯

E

F

F♯/G♭

G

A♭/G♯

Other Chords

G7sus4
G Dominant 7th sus4

(1st position)

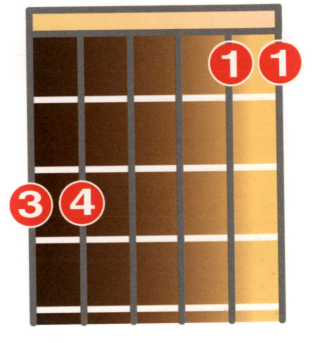

Chord Spelling

1st (G), 4th (C), 5th (D), ♭7th (F)

A

B♭/A#

B

C

C#/D♭

D

E♭/D#

E

F

F#/G♭

G

A♭/G#

Other
Chords

G7sus4
G Dominant 7th sus4

(2nd position)

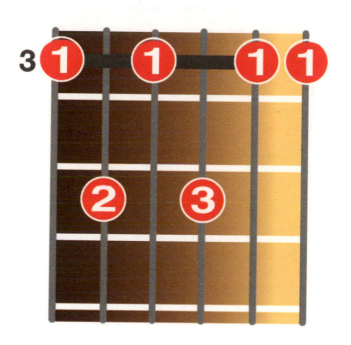

Chord Spelling

1st (G), 4th (C), 5th (D), ♭7th (F)

A
B♭/A♯
B
C
C♯/D♭
D
E♭/D♯
E
F
F♯/G♭
G
A♭/G♯
Other Chords

G6
G Major 6th
(1st position)

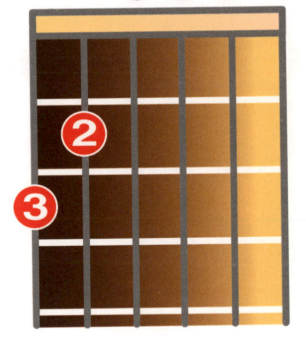

Chord Spelling
1st (G), 3rd (B), 5th (D), 6th (E)

A

B♭/A♯

B

C

C♯/D♭

D

E♭/D♯

E

F

F♯/G♭

G

A♭/G♯

Other
Chords

G6
G Major 6th
(2nd position)

O

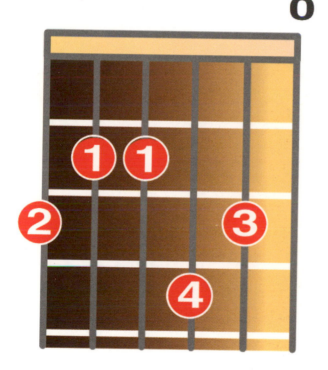

Chord Spelling

1st (G), 3rd (B), 5th (D), 6th (E)

A

Bb/A#

B

C

C#/Db

D

Eb/D#

E

F

F#/Gb

G

Ab/G#

Other Chords

Gm6
G Minor 6th
(1st position)

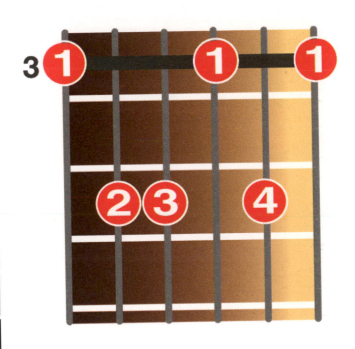

A
B♭/A♯
B
C
C♯/D♭
D
E♭/D♯
E
F
F♯/G♭
G
A♭/G♯
Other Chords

3

Chord Spelling

1st (G), ♭3rd (B♭), 5th (D), 6th (E)

Gm6
G Minor 6th
(2nd position)

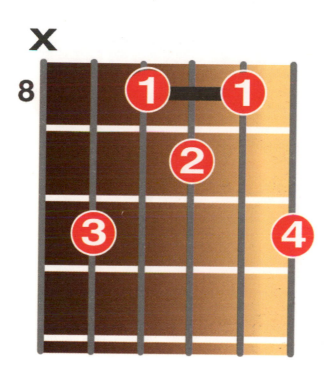

X

8

A
B♭/A♯
B
C
C♯/D♭
D
E♭/D♯
E
F
F♯/G♭
G
A♭/G♯
Other Chords

Chord Spelling
1st (G), ♭3rd (B♭), 5th (D), 6th (E)

G7
G Dominant 7th

(1st position)

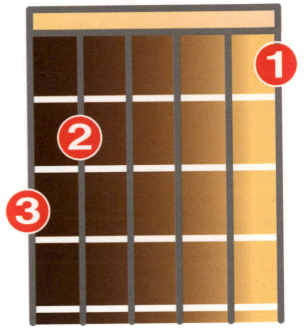

Chord Spelling

1st (G), 3rd (B), 5th (D), ♭7th (F)

A
B♭/A♯
B
C
C♯/D♭
D
E♭/D♯
E
F
F♯/G♭
G
A♭/G♯
Other Chords

G7
G Dominant 7th
(2nd position)

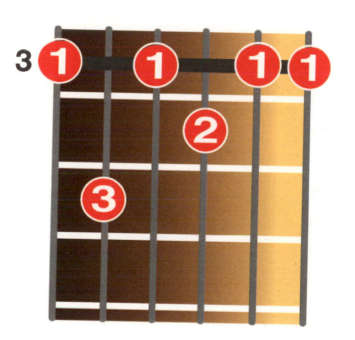

A
B♭/A♯
B
C
C♯/D♭
D
E♭/D♯
E
F
F♯/G♭
G
A♭/G♯
Other Chords

Chord Spelling
1st (G), 3rd (B), 5th (D), ♭7th (F)

G9
G Dominant 9th
(1st position)

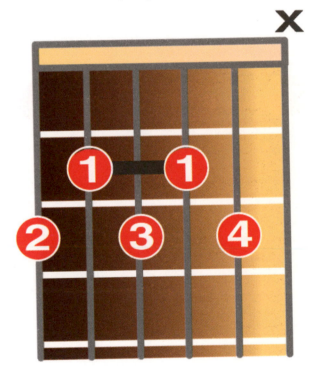

Chord Spelling

1st (G), 3rd (B), 5th (D), ♭7th (F), 9th (A)

A

B♭/A♯

B

C

C♯/D♭

D

E♭/D♯

E

F

F♯/G♭

G

A♭/G♯

Other
Chords

G9
G Dominant 9th
(2nd position)

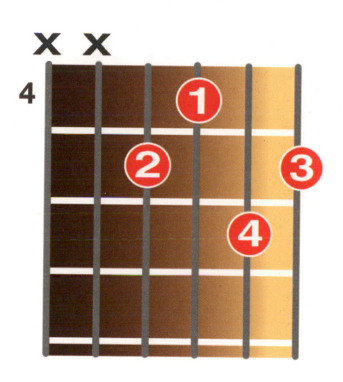

A
B♭/A♯
B
C
C♯/D♭
D
E♭/D♯
E
F
F♯/G♭
G
A♭/G♯
Other Chords

Chord Spelling
1st (G), 3rd (B), 5th (D), ♭7th (F), 9th (A)

G5

G 5th 'power chord'

(1st position)

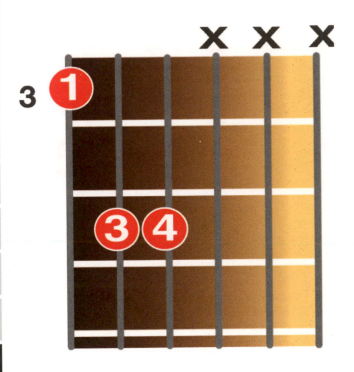

Chord Spelling

1st (G), 5th (D)

G⁶₉
G Major 6th add 9th

(1st position)

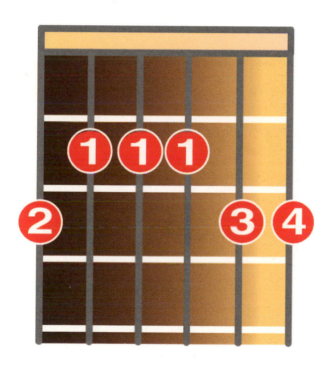

A
B♭/A♯
B
C
C♯/D♭
D
E♭/D♯
E
F
F♯/G♭
G
A♭/G♯
Other Chords

Chord Spelling

1st (G), 3rd (B), 5th (D), 6th (E), 9th (A)

G11
G Dominant 11th

(1st position)

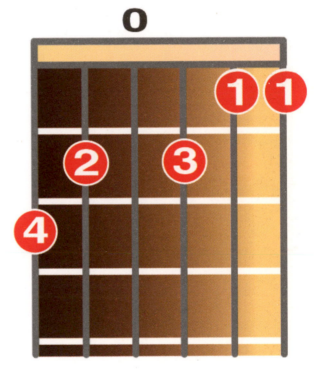

A
B♭/A♯
B
C
C♯/D♭
D
E♭/D♯
E
F
F♯/G♭
G
A♭/G♯
Other Chords

Chord Spelling

1st (G), 3rd (B), 5th (D), ♭7th (F), 9th (A), 11th (C)

G13

G Dominant 13th

(1st position)

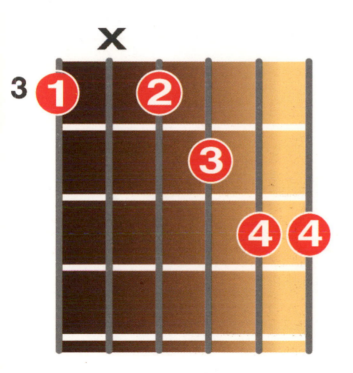

A
Bb/A#
B
C
C#/Db
D
Eb/D#
E
F
F#/Gb
G
Ab/G#
Other Chords

Chord Spelling

1st (G), 3rd (B), 5th (D), ♭7th (F), 9th (A), 13th (E)

Gadd9
G Major add 9th

(1st position)

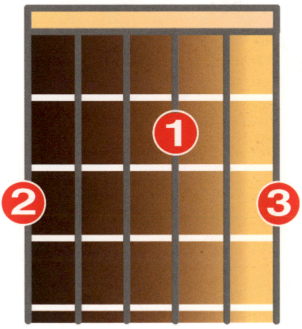

Chord Spelling

1st (G), 3rd (B), 5th (D), 9th (A)

A
B♭/A♯
B
C
C♯/D♭
D
E♭/D♯
E
F
F♯/G♭
G
A♭/G♯
Other Chords

Gm9
G Minor 9th
(1st position)

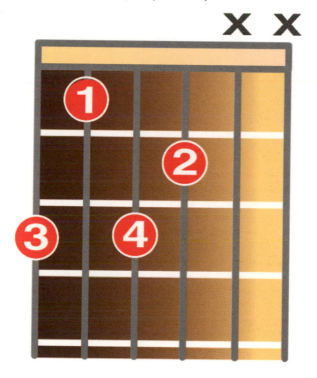

A
B♭/A♯
B
C
C♯/D♭
D
E♭/D♯
E
F
F♯/G♭
G
A♭/G♯
Other Chords

Chord Spelling

1st (G), ♭3rd (B♭), 5th (D), ♭7th (F), 9th (A)

Gmaj9
G Major 9th

(1st position)

A
B♭/A♯
B
C
C♯/D♭
D
E♭/D♯
E
F
F♯/G♭
G
A♭/G♯
Other Chords

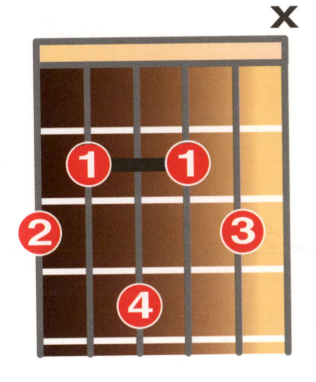

Chord Spelling

1st (G), 3rd (B), 5th (D), 7th (F♯), 9th (A)

G+
G Augmented
(1st position)

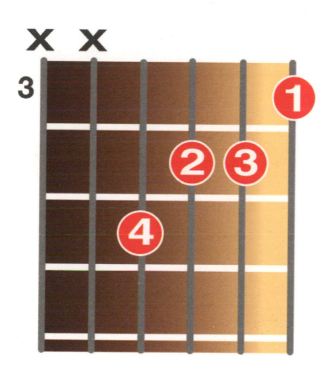

A
B♭/A♯
B
C
C♯/D♭
D
E♭/D♯
E
F
F♯/G♭
G
A♭/G♯
Other Chords

Chord Spelling
1st (G), 3rd (B), #5th (D#)

G^{o7}

G Diminished 7th

(1st position)

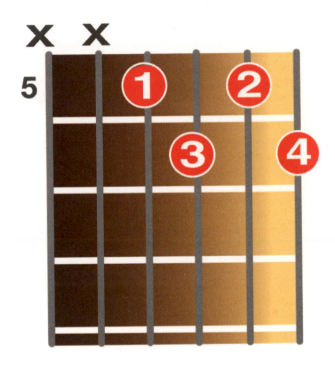

Chord Spelling

1st (G), ♭3rd (B♭), ♭5th (D♭), ♭♭7th (F♭)

G⁰
G Diminished triad

(1st position)

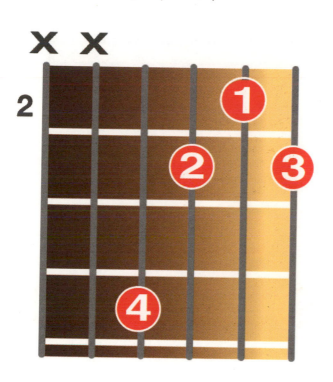

A

B♭/A♯

B

C

C♯/D♭

D

E♭/D♯

E

F

F♯/G♭

G

A♭/G♯

Other Chords

Chord Spelling

1st (G), ♭3rd (B♭), ♭5th (D♭)

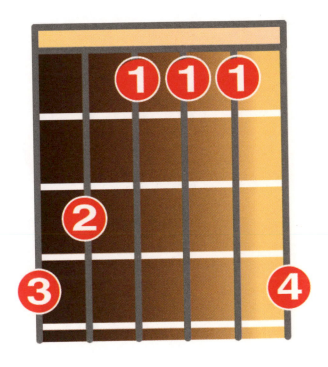

A♭

A♭ Major

(1st position)

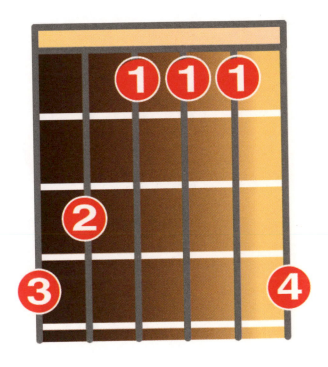

A
B♭/A♯
B
C
C♯/D♭
D
E♭/D♯
E
F
F♯/G♭
G
A♭/G♯
Other Chords

Chord Spelling

1st (A♭), 3rd (C), 5th (E♭)

A♭

A♭ Major

(2nd position)

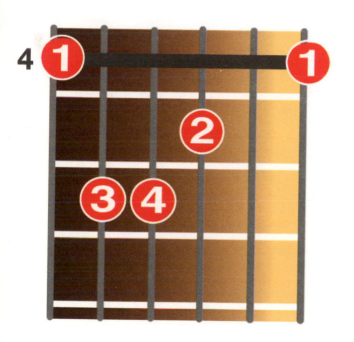

A

B♭/A♯

B

C

C♯/D♭

D

E♭/D♯

E

F

F♯/G♭

G

A♭/G♯

Other Chords

Chord Spelling

1st (A♭), 3rd (C), 5th (E♭)

A♭m
A♭ Minor

(1st position)

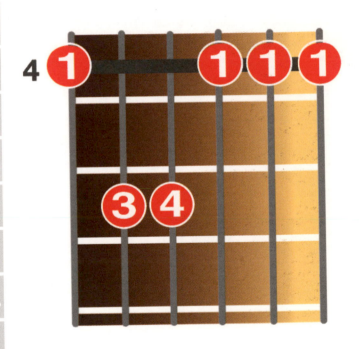

Chord Spelling

1st (A♭), ♭3rd (C♭), 5th (E♭)

A

B♭/A♯

B

C

C♯/D♭

D

E♭/D♯

E

F

F♯/G♭

G

A♭/G♯

Other
Chords

A♭m
A♭ Minor
(2nd position)

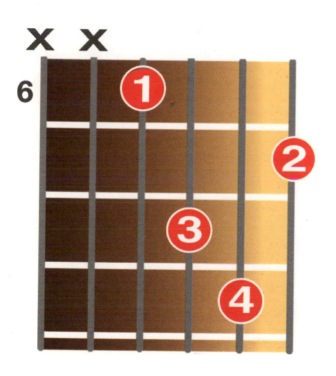

X X

6

1
2
3
4

A
B♭/A♯
B
C
C♯/D♭
D
E♭/D♯
E
F
F♯/G♭
G
A♭/G♯
Other Chords

Chord Spelling
1st (A♭), ♭3rd (C♭), 5th (E♭)

A♭maj7
A♭ Major 7th
(1st position)

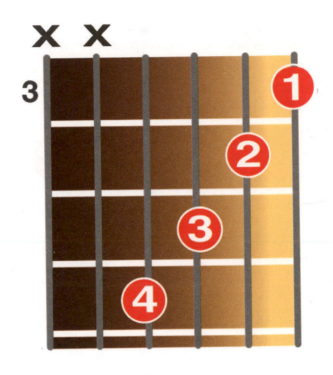

Chord Spelling
1st (A♭), 3rd (C), 5th (E♭), 7th (G)

A♭maj7
A♭ Major 7th
(2nd position)

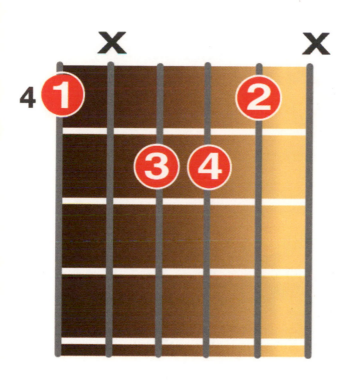

Chord Spelling
1st (A♭), 3rd (C), 5th (E♭), 7th (G)

A

B♭/A♯

B

C

C♯/D♭

D

E♭/D♯

E

F

F♯/G♭

G

A♭/G♯

Other Chords

A♭m7
A♭ Minor 7th

(1st position)

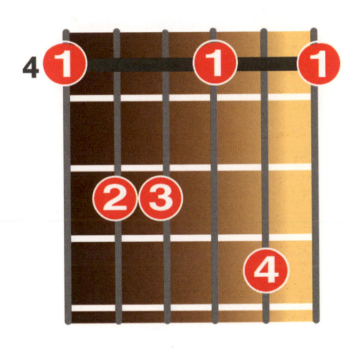

Chord Spelling

1st (A♭), ♭3rd (C♭), 5th (E♭), ♭7th (G♭)

A♭m7
A♭ Minor 7th
(2nd position)

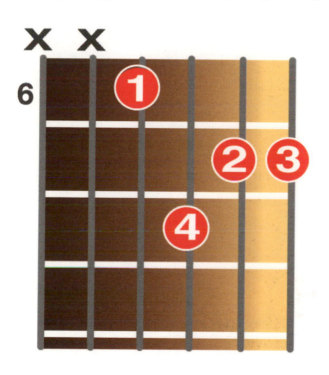

A
B♭/A♯
B
C
C♯/D♭
D
E♭/D♯
E
F
F♯/G♭
G
A♭/G♯
Other Chords

Chord Spelling

1st (A♭), ♭3rd (C♭), 5th (E♭), ♭7th (G♭)

A♭sus4
A♭ Suspended 4th
(1st position)

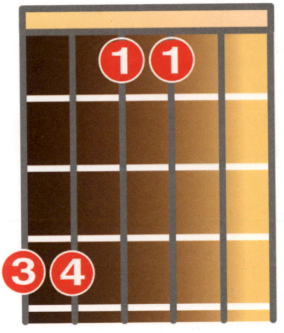

Chord Spelling
1st (A♭), 4th (D♭), 5th (E♭)

A♭sus4
A♭ Suspended 4th
(2nd position)

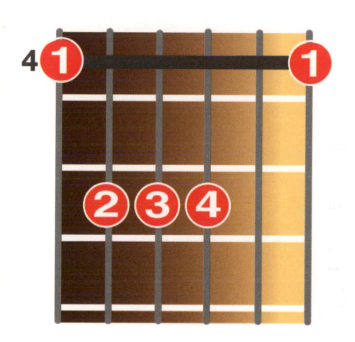

Chord Spelling

1st (A♭), 4th (D♭), 5th (E♭)

A

B♭/A♯

B

C

C♯/D♭

D

E♭/D♯

E

F

F♯/G♭

G

A♭/G♯

Other Chords

A♭7sus4

A♭ Dominant 7th sus4

(1st position)

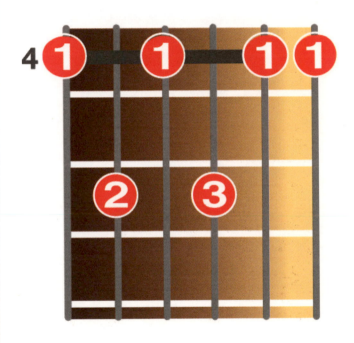

Chord Spelling

1st (A♭), 4th (D♭), 5th (E♭), 7th (G♭)

A♭7sus4

A♭ Dominant 7th sus4

(2nd position)

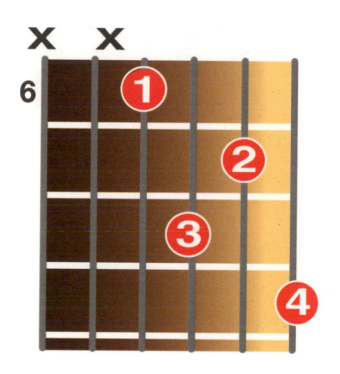

A

B♭/A♯

B

C

C♯/D♭

D

E♭/D♯

E

F

F♯/G♭

G

A♭/G♯

Other Chords

Chord Spelling

1st (A♭), 4th (D♭), 5th (E♭), 7th (G♭)

A♭6
A♭ Major 6th
(1st position)

A
B♭/A#
B
C
C#/D♭
D
E♭/D#
E
F
F#/G♭
G
A♭/G#
Other Chords

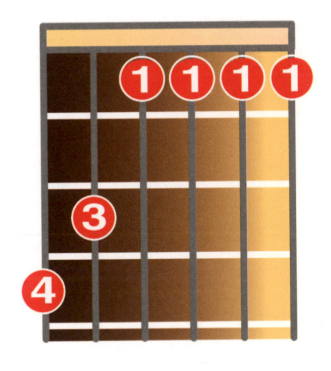

Chord Spelling
1st (A♭), 3rd (C), 5th (E♭), 6th (F)

A♭6
A♭ Major 6th
(2nd position)

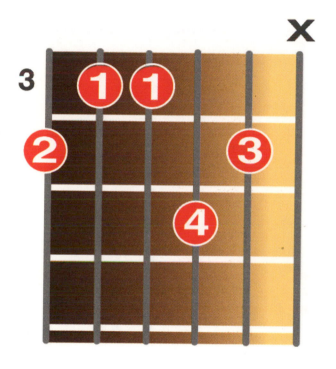

Chord Spelling

1st (A♭), 3rd (C), 5th (E♭), 6th (F)

A

B♭/A#

B

C

C#/D♭

D

E♭/D#

E

F

F#/G♭

G

A♭/G#

Other Chords

A♭m6

A♭ Minor 6th

(1st position)

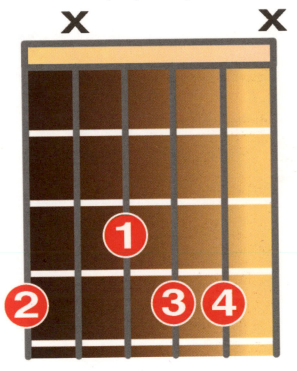

Chord Spelling

1st (A♭), ♭3rd (C♭), 5th (E♭), 6th (F)

A
B♭/A#
B
C
C#/D♭
D
E♭/D#
E
F
F#/G♭
G
A♭/G#
Other Chords

A♭m6
A♭ Minor 6th
(2nd position)

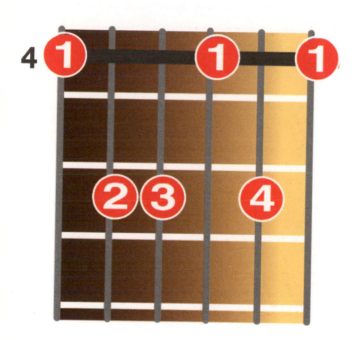

A
B♭/A#
B
C
C#/D♭
D
E♭/D#
E
F
F#/G♭
G
A♭/G#
Other Chords

Chord Spelling

1st (A♭), ♭3rd (C♭), 5th (E♭), 6th (F)

A♭7

A♭ Dominant 7th

(1st position)

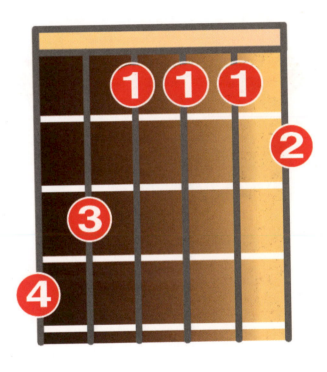

Chord Spelling

1st (A♭), 3rd (C), 5th (E♭), ♭7th (G♭)

A

B♭/A#

B

C

C#/D♭

D

E♭/D#

E

F

F#/G♭

G

A♭/G#

Other Chords

A♭7
A♭ Dominant 7th
(2nd position)

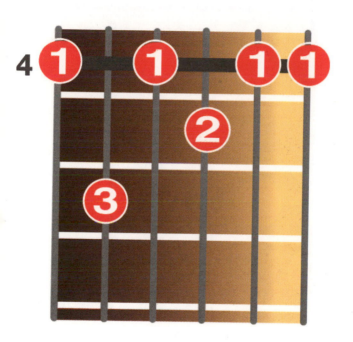

A
B♭/A♯
B
C
C♯/D♭
D
E♭/D♯
E
F
F♯/G♭
G
A♭/G♯
Other Chords

Chord Spelling

1st (A♭), 3rd (C), 5th (E♭), ♭7th (G♭)

A♭9

A♭ Dominant 9th

(1st position)

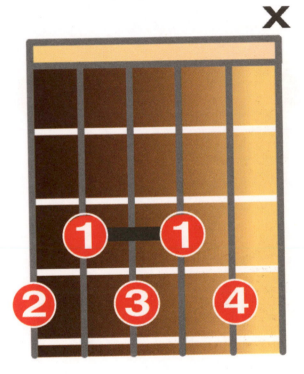

Chord Spelling

1st (A♭), 3rd (C), 5th (E♭), ♭7th (G♭), 9th (B)

A♭9

A♭ Dominant 9th

(2nd position)

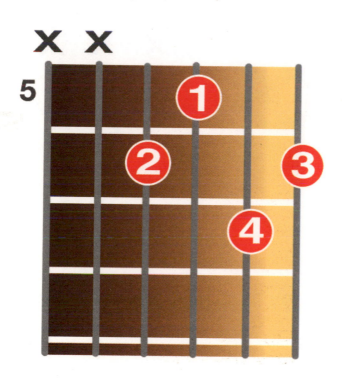

Chord Spelling

1st (A♭), 3rd (C), 5th (E♭), ♭7th (G♭), 9th (B)

A

B♭/A♯

B

C

C♯/D♭

D

E♭/D♯

E

F

F♯/G♭

G

A♭/G♯

Other Chords

A♭5

A♭ 5th 'power chord'

(1st position)

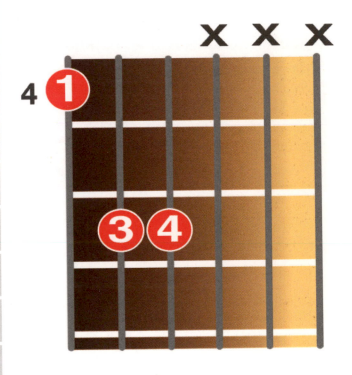

A
B♭/A#
B
C
C#/D♭
D
E♭/D#
E
F
F#/G♭
G
A♭/G#
Other Chords

Chord Spelling

1st (A♭), 5th (E♭)

A♭⁶₉

A♭ Major 6th add 9th

(1st position)

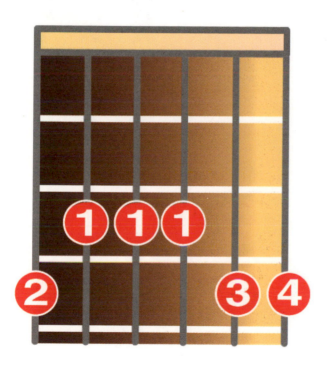

Chord Spelling

1st (A♭), 3rd (C), 5th (E♭), 6th (F), 9th (B♭)

A
B♭/A#
B
C
C#/D♭
D
E♭/D#
E
F
F#/G♭
G
A♭/G#
Other Chords

A♭11

A♭ Dominant 11th

(1st position)

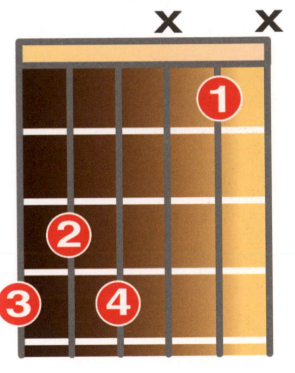

Chord Spelling

1st (A♭), 3rd (C), 5th (E♭), ♭7th (G♭), 9th (B♭), 11th (D♭)

A

B♭/A♯

B

C

C♯/D♭

D

E♭/D♯

E

F

F♯/G♭

G

A♭/G♯

Other Chords

A♭13

A♭ Dominant 13th

(1st position)

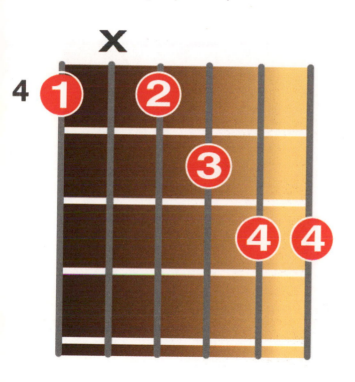

Chord Spelling

st (A♭), 3rd (C), 5th (E♭), ♭7th (G♭), 9th (B♭), 13th (F)

A

B♭/A♯

B

C

C♯/D♭

D

E♭/D♯

E

F

F♯/G♭

G

A♭/G♯

Other Chords

A♭add9
A♭ Major add 9th

(1st position)

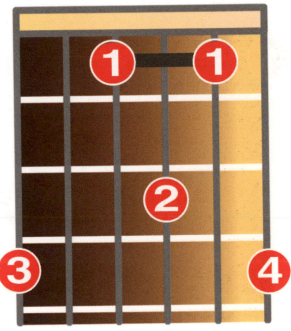

Chord Spelling

1st (A♭), 3rd (C), 5th (E♭), 9th (B♭)

A♭m9
A♭ Minor 9th
(1st position)

A

B♭/A♯

B

C

C♯/D♭

D

E♭/D♯

E

F

F♯/G♭

G

A♭/G♯

Other Chords

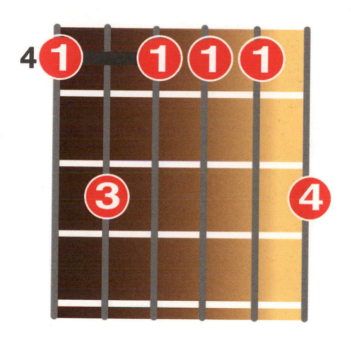

Chord Spelling

1st (A♭), ♭3rd (C♭), 5th (E♭), ♭7th (G♭), 9th (B♭)

A♭maj9
A♭ Major 9th

(1st position)

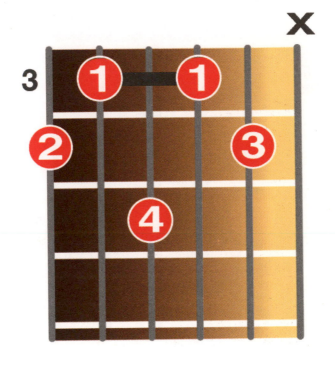

Chord Spelling

1st (A♭), 3rd (C), 5th (E♭), 7th (G), 9th (B♭)

A♭+

A♭ Augmented

(1st position)

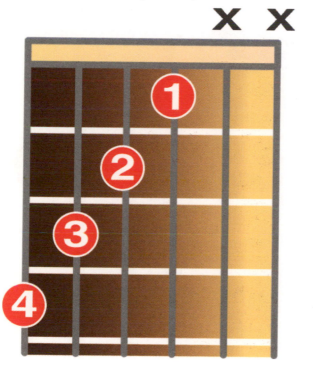

Chord Spelling

1st (A♭), 3rd (C), #5th (E)

A

B♭/A♯

B

C

C♯/D♭

D

E♭/D♯

E

F

F♯/G♭

G

A♭/G♯

Other Chords

A♭⁰⁷

A♭ Diminished 7th

(1st position)

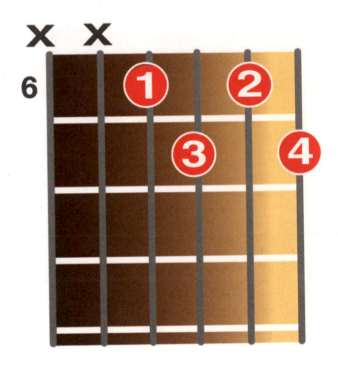

Chord Spelling

1st (A♭), ♭3rd (C♭), ♭5th (E♭♭), ♭♭7th (G♭♭)

A♭⁰

A♭ Diminished triad

(1st position)

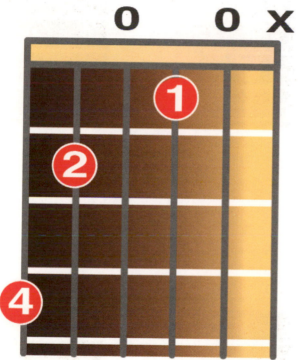

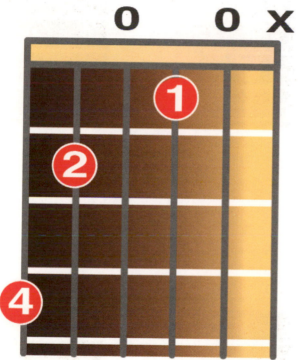

O   O X

Chord Spelling

1st (A♭), ♭3rd (C♭), ♭5th (E♭♭)

A

B♭/A♯

B

C

C♯/D♭

D

E♭/D♯

E

F

F♯/G♭

G

A♭/G♯

Other Chords

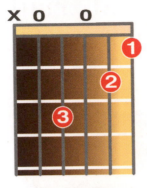

A7#5
A Dominant 7th #5
(1st position)

Chord Spelling
1st (A), 3rd (C#), #5th (E#), ♭7th (G)

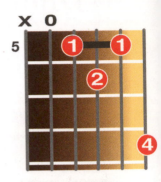

A7#9
A Dominant 7th #9
(1st position)

Chord Spelling
1st (A), 3rd (C#), 5th (E), ♭7th (G), #9th

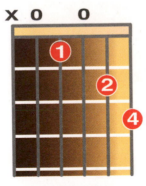

A7♭5
A Dominant 7th ♭5
(1st position)

Chord Spelling
1st (A), 3rd (C#), ♭5th (E♭), ♭7th (G)

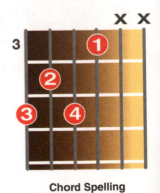

A7♭9
A Dominant 7th ♭9
(1st position)

Chord Spelling
1st (A), 3rd (C#), 5th (E), ♭7th (G), ♭9th

A
B♭/A#
B
C
C#/D♭
D
E♭/D#
E
F
F#/G♭
G
A♭/G#
Other Chords

A9♭5

A Dominant 9th ♭5

(1st position)

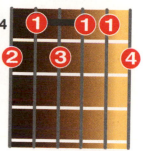

Chord Spelling

(A), 3rd (C♯), ♭5th (E♭), ♭7th (G), 9th (B)

B♭7♯5

B♭ Dominant 7th ♯5

(1st position)

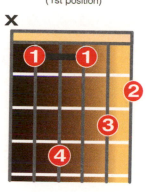

Chord Spelling

1st (B♭), 3rd (D), ♯5th (F♯), ♭7th (A♭)

B♭7♯9

B♭ Dominant 7th ♯9

(1st position)

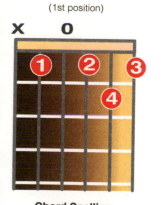

Chord Spelling

(B♭), 3rd (D), 5th (F), ♭7th (A♭), ♯9th (C♯)

B♭7♭5

B♭ Dominant 7th ♭5

(1st position)

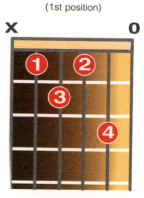

Chord Spelling

1st (B♭), 3rd (D), ♭5th (F♭), ♭7th (A♭)

A

B♭/A♯

B

C

C♯/D♭

D

E♭/D♯

E

F

F♯/G♭

G

A♭/G♯

Other Chords

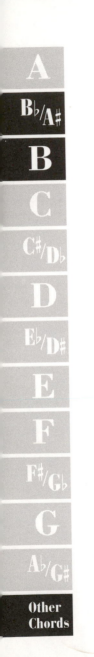

B♭7♭9
B♭ Dominant 7th ♭9
(1st position)

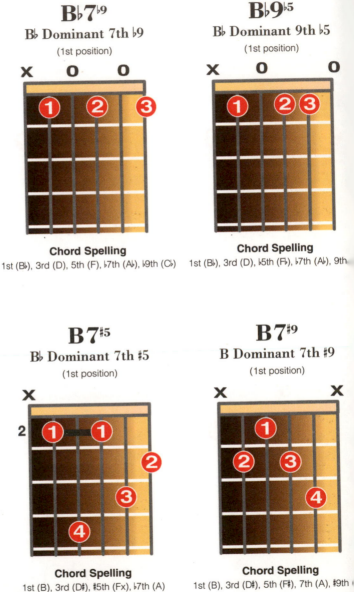

Chord Spelling
1st (B♭), 3rd (D), 5th (F), ♭7th (A♭), ♭9th (C♭)

B♭9♭5
B♭ Dominant 9th ♭5
(1st position)

Chord Spelling
1st (B♭), 3rd (D), ♭5th (F♭), ♭7th (A♭), 9th

B7♯5
B♭ Dominant 7th ♯5
(1st position)

Chord Spelling
1st (B), 3rd (D♯), ♯5th (Fx), ♭7th (A)

B7♯9
B Dominant 7th ♯9
(1st position)

Chord Spelling
1st (B), 3rd (D♯), 5th (F♯), 7th (A), ♯9th

B7♭5
B Dominant 7th ♭5
(1st position)

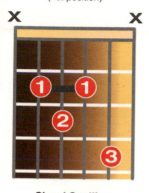

Chord Spelling
1st (B), 3rd (D♯), ♭5th (F), ♭7th (A)

B7♭9
B Dominant 7th ♭9
(1st position)

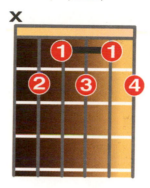

Chord Spelling
1st (B), 3rd (D♯), 5th (F♯), ♭7th (A), ♭9th (C)

B9♭5
B Dominant 9th ♭5
(1st position)

Chord Spelling
(B), 3rd (D♯), ♭5th (F), ♭7th (A), 9th (C♯)

C7♯5
C Dominant 7th ♯5
(1st position)

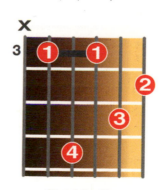

Chord Spelling
1st (C), 3rd (E), ♯5th (G♯), ♭7th (B♭)

A

B♭/A♯

B

C

C♯/D♭

D

E♭/D♯

E

F

F♯/G♭

G

A♭/G♯

Other Chords

A

B♭/A♯

B

C

C♯/D♭

D

E♭/D♯

E

F

F♯/G♭

G

A♭/G♯

Other
Chords

C7♯9

C Dominant 7th ♯9

(1st position)

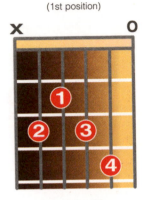

Chord Spelling

1st (C), 3rd (E), 5th (G), ♭7th (B♭), ♯9th (D♯)

C7♭5

C Dominant 7th ♭5

(1st position)

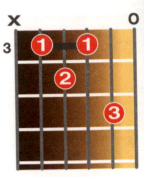

Chord Spelling

1st (C), 3rd (E), ♭5th (G♭), ♭7th (B♭)

C7♭9

C Dominant 7th ♭9

(1st position)

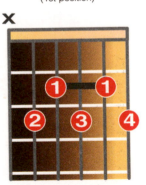

Chord Spelling

1st (C), 3rd (E), 5th (G), ♭7th (B♭), ♭9th (D♭)

C9♭5

C Dominant 9th ♭5

(1st position)

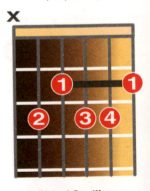

Chord Spelling

1st (C), 3rd (E), ♭5th (G♭), ♭7th (B♭), 9th

C#7#5

C# Dominant 7th #5

(1st position)

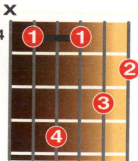

Chord Spelling

1st (C#), 3rd (E#), #5th (Gx), ♭7th (B)

C#7#9

C# Dominant 7th #9

(1st position)

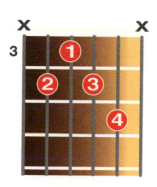

Chord Spelling

1st (C#), 3rd (E#), 5th (G#), ♭7th (B), #9th (Dx)

C#7♭5

C# Dominant 7th ♭5

(1st position)

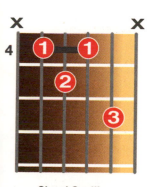

Chord Spelling

1st (C#), 3rd (E#), ♭5th (G), ♭7th (B)

C#7♭9

C# Dominant 7th ♭9

(1st position)

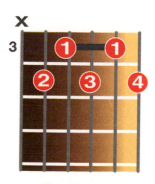

Chord Spelling

1st (C#), 3rd (E#), 5th (G#), ♭7th (B), ♭9th (D)

A

B♭/A#

B

C

C#/D♭

D

E♭/D#

E

F

F#/G♭

G

A♭/G#

Other Chords

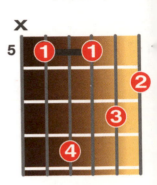

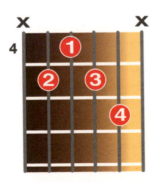

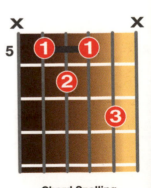

C#9♭5
C# Dominant 9th ♭5
(1st position)

Chord Spelling
1st (C#), 3rd (E#), ♭5th (G), ♭7th (B), 9th (D#)

D7#5
D Dominant 7th #5
(1st position)

Chord Spelling
1st (D), 3rd (F#), #5th (A#), ♭7th (C)

D7#9
D Dominant 7th #9
(1st position)

Chord Spelling
1st (D), 3rd (F#), 5th (A), ♭7th (C), #9th (E#)

D7♭5
D Dominant 7th ♭5
(1st position)

Chord Spelling
1st (D), 3rd (F#), ♭5th (A♭), ♭7th (C)

A
B♭/A#
B
C
C#/D♭
D
E♭/D#
E
F
F#/G♭
G
A♭/G#
Other Chords

D7♭9

D Dominant 7th ♭9

(1st position)

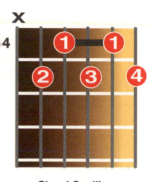

Chord Spelling

1st (D), 3rd (F♯), 5th (A), ♭7th (C), ♭9th (E♭)

D9♭5

D Dominant 9th ♭5

(1st position)

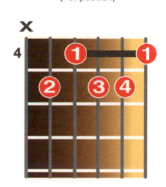

Chord Spelling

1st (D), 3rd (F♯), ♭5th (A♭), ♭7th (C), 9th (E)

E♭7♯5

E♭ Dominant 7th ♯5

(1st position)

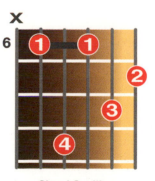

Chord Spelling

1st (E♭), 3rd (G), ♯5th (B), ♭7th (D♭)

E♭7♯9

E♭ Dominant 7th ♯9

(1st position)

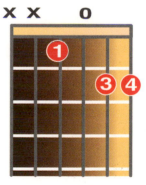

Chord Spelling

1st (E♭), 3rd (G), 5th (B♭), ♭7th (D♭), ♯9th (F♯)

A

B♭/A♯

B

C

C♯/D♭

D

E♭/D♯

E

F

F♯/G♭

G

A♭/G♯

Other
Chords

E♭7♭5
E♭ Dominant 7th ♭5
(1st position)

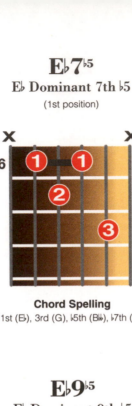

Chord Spelling
1st (E♭), 3rd (G), ♭5th (B♭♭), ♭7th (D♭)

E♭7♭9
E♭ Dominant 7th ♭9
(1st position)

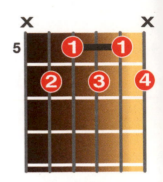

Chord Spelling
1st (E♭), 3rd (G), 5th (B♭), ♭7th (D♭), ♭9th

E♭9♭5
E♭ Dominant 9th ♭5
(1st position)

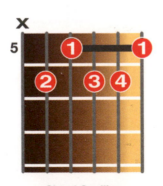

Chord Spelling
1st (E♭), 3rd (G), ♭5th (B♭♭), ♭7th (D♭), 9th (F)

E7♯5
E Dominant 7th ♯5
(1st position)

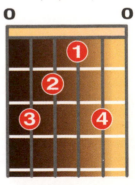

Chord Spelling
1st (E), 3rd (G♯), ♯5th (B♯), ♭7th (D)

A
B♭/A♯
B
C
C♯/D♭
D
E♭/D♯
E
F
F♯/G♭
G
A♭/G♯
Other Chords

E7♯9

E Dominant 7th ♯9

(1st position)

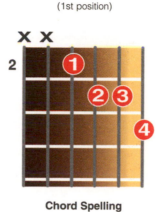

Chord Spelling

(E), 3rd (G♯), 5th (B), ♭7th (D), ♯9th (Fx)

E7♭5

E Dominant 7th ♭5

(1st position)

Chord Spelling

1st (E), 3rd (G♯), ♭5th (B♭), ♭7th (D)

E7♭9

E Dominant 7th ♭9

(1st position)

Chord Spelling

(E), 3rd (G♯), 5th (B), ♭7th (D), ♭9th (F)

E9♭5

E Dominant 9th ♭5

(1st position)

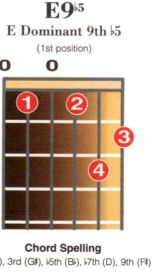

Chord Spelling

1st (E), 3rd (G♯), ♭5th (B♭), ♭7th (D), 9th (F♯)

A

B♭/A♯

B

C

C♯/D♭

D

E♭/D♯

E

F

F♯/G♭

G

A♭/G♯

Other
Chords

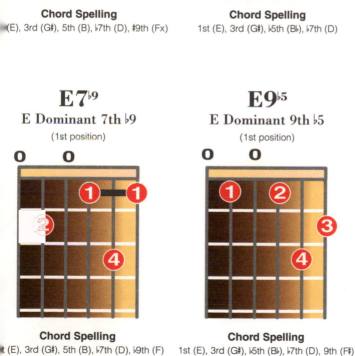

A

B♭/A♯

B

C

C♯/D♭

D

E♭/D♯

E

F

F♯/G♭

G

A♭/G♯

Other
Chords

F7♯5
F Dominant 7th ♯5
(1st position)

Chord Spelling
1st (F), 3rd (A), ♯5th (C♯), ♭7th (E♭)

F7♯9
F Dominant 7th ♯9
(1st position)

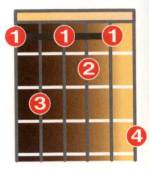

Chord Spelling
1st (F), 3rd (A), 5th (C), ♭7th (E♭), ♯9th (

F7♭5
F Dominant 7th ♭5
(1st position)

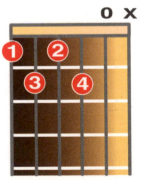

Chord Spelling
1st (F), 3rd (A), ♭5th (C♭), ♭7th (E♭)

F7♭9
F Dominant 7th ♭9
(1st position)

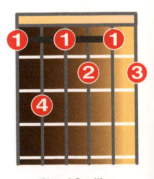

Chord Spelling
1st (F), 3rd (A), 5th (C), ♭7th (E♭), ♭9th (

F9♭5

F Dominant 9th ♭5

(1st position)

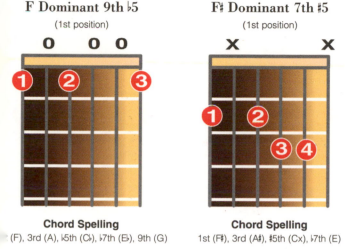

Chord Spelling
(F), 3rd (A), ♭5th (C♭), ♭7th (E♭), 9th (G)

F♯7♯5

F♯ Dominant 7th ♯5

(1st position)

Chord Spelling
1st (F♯), 3rd (A♯), ♯5th (Cx), ♭7th (E)

F♯7♯9

F♯ Dominant 7th ♯9

(1st position)

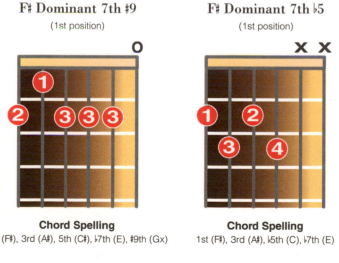

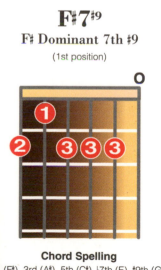

Chord Spelling
(F♯), 3rd (A♯), 5th (C♯), ♭7th (E), ♯9th (Gx)

F♯7♭5

F♯ Dominant 7th ♭5

(1st position)

Chord Spelling
1st (F♯), 3rd (A♯), ♭5th (C), ♭7th (E)

A

B♭/A♯

B

C

C♯/D♭

D

E♭/D♯

E

F

F♯/G♭

G

A♭/G♯

Other Chords

A

B♭/A♯

B

C

C♯/D♭

D

E♭/D♯

E

F

F♯/G♭

G

A♭/G♯

Other
Chords

F♯7♭9

F♯ Dominant 7th ♭9

(1st position)

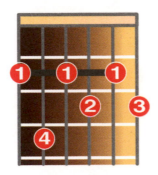

Chord Spelling
1st (F♯), 3rd (A♯), 5th (C♯), ♭7th (E), ♭9th (G)

F♯9♭5

F♯ Dominant 9th ♭5

(1st position)

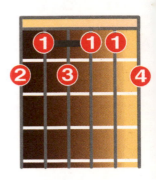

Chord Spelling
1st (F♯), 3rd (A♯), ♭5th (C), ♭7th (E), 9th (

G7♯5

G Dominant 7th ♯5

(1st position)

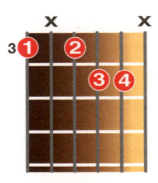

Chord Spelling
1st (G), 3rd (B), ♯5th (D♯), ♭7th (F)

G7♯9

G Dominant 7th ♯9

(1st position)

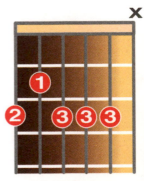

Chord Spelling
1st (G), 3rd (B), 5th (D), ♭7th (F), ♯9th (A

G7♭5

G Dominant 7th ♭5

(1st position)

X X

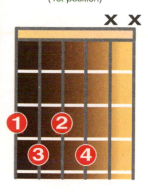

Chord Spelling
1st (G), 3rd (B), ♭5th (D♭), ♭7th (F)

G7♭9

G Dominant 7th ♭9

(1st position)

O X

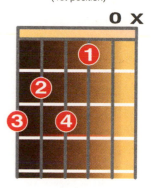

Chord Spelling
1st (G), 3rd (B), 5th (D), ♭7th (F), ♭9th (A♭)

G9♭5

G Dominant 9th ♭5

(1st position)

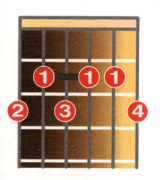

Chord Spelling
1st (G), 3rd (B), ♭5th (D♭), ♭7th (F), 9th (A)

A♭7♯5

A♭ Dominant 7th ♯5

(1st position)

X X

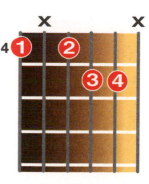

Chord Spelling
1st (A♭), 3rd (C), ♯5th (E)

A

B♭/A♯

B

C

C♯/D♭

D

E♭/D♯

E

F

F♯/G♭

G

A♭/G♯

Other Chords

A

B♭/A♯

B

C

C♯/D♭

D

E♭/D♯

E

F

F♯/G♭

G

A♭/G♯

Other
Chords

A♭7♯9
A♭ Dominant 7th #9
(1st position)

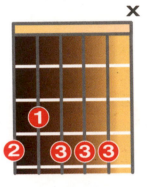

Chord Spelling
1st (A♭), 3rd (C), 5th (E♭), ♭7th (G♭), #9th (B)

A♭7♭5
A♭ Dominant 7th ♭5
(1st position)

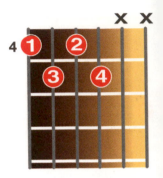

Chord Spelling
1st (A♭), 3rd (C), ♭5th (E♭♭), ♭7th (G♭)

A♭7♭9
A♭ Dominant 7th ♭9
(1st position)

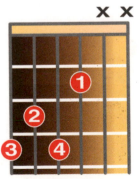

Chord Spelling
1st (A♭), 3rd (C), 5th (E♭), ♭7th (G♭), ♭9th (B♭♭)

A♭9♭5
A♭ Dominant 9th ♭5
(1st position)

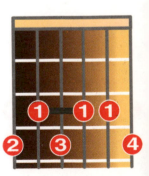

Chord Spelling
1st (A♭), 3rd (C), ♭5th (E♭♭), ♭7th (G♭), 9th

Some Notes About Chords

Chord Chart

This is the most commonly used method of notating a chord progression. Each bar is indicated by a vertical line (with two lines at the end). Chords are indicated by chord symbols. Where two or more chords occur within a single bar, the division is shown by a dot or diagonal line after each chord to indicate another beat. If no such signs occur then the bar can be assumed to be evenly divided between the chords that appear within it.

Triads

Triads are basic three-note chords that are also the building blocks of all other chords. There are four basic triads: a major triad is the first, third and fifth notes of the diatonic major scale (C, E and G in the key of C); a minor triad is the first third and fifth notes of the natural minor scale (C, Eb and G in the key of C); an augmented triad is a major triad with a sharpened fifth note (C, E and GI in the key of C); and a diminished triad is a minor triad with a flattened fifth note (C, Eb and Gb in the key of C). All of these basic chords can be extended; a major seventh chord, for example, is a major triad with a seventh note added (C, E, G and B in the key of C).

Open Chords

These are chords in which open strings are used as part of the chord. They are normally, but not exclusively, played at the nut end of the fretboard. They are more often used in acoustic rather than electric guitar playing.

Barre Chords

These are chords in which no open strings are played –
instead the first finger lies flat across all the strings. Barre
chord shapes are just open-position chords re-fingered,
thereby leaving the first finger free for holding the barre.
The advantage of barre chords is that once you have learned
one shape, you can use it for all of the 12 different keys
simply by moving it up or down the neck to change the pitch.
This can be especially useful when playing rhythm guitar.
As barre chords do not involve open strings they can sound
great with distortion, and are well suited for use with punchy
rhythmic techniques (like staccato). The most common barre
chords are the 'E' and 'A' shapes based on the E and A open
chords respectively. When playing a barre chord, ensure that
the first finger is close to, and in line with, the fret rather
than at an angle to it.

Partial-Barre Chords

These are chords in which the top two, three or four strings
are fretted with the first finger. The first finger must lie flat
across the strings in order for them to sound clearly; any
other fingers that are used should fret strings with their tips.
Partial-barre chords are sometimes used in place of full-
barre chords in order to achieve a crisper and lighter sound.

FLAME TREE PUBLISHING, Crabtree Hall,
Crabtree Lane, Fulham, London, SW6 6TY
United Kingdom. www.flametreepublishing.com
See our music information site: www.musicfirebox.com